ainless Fir   y

A Guide for Business Owners & Managers

Painless Financial
TRAINING GROUP

Debi J. Peverill CA

Painless Financial Literacy: A Guide for Business Owners & Managers

By Debi J. Peverill CA

ISBN 978-0-9917872-2-7

Copyright MMXV Painless Financial Training Group Inc.

Published by PFTGI
Suite 206, 15 Dartmouth Road
Bedford, Nova Scotia
B4A 3X6

Printed in Canada

CONTENTS

Read This First

This book is all about helping you understand accounting and finance rules so you can make the best financial decisions.

When I wrote the book I struggled with what topics to put first and which concepts had to be defined and explained before the other concepts would make any sense. In the end, this is how I decided to put it together, because it's my book. But you can read the book in any order. You can read the sections that interest you the most, then go back and read the rest, or not!

The financial world has been vastly complicated by recent changes in generally accepted accounting principles (GAAP). There is now a separate set of accounting principles for public companies, owner managed companies, and non-profit organizations (NPOs).

So the first thing you might want to do is figure out which set of rules are most likely to apply to the financial decisions you are making. Do you own a business? If so, you care about the rules for owner managed companies. If you work for a NPO, then the accounting standards for NPOs will be the most relevant. A lot of the basic stuff is the same for private, public and NPOs, but where there are differences I have mentioned them. There will be parts of the book that do not apply to you.

The book has a lot of content and if you don't have much familiarity with things financial, it might seem a little daunting at the beginning. But keep reading and I promise you it will all make sense by the end of the book.

Chapter 1. Financial Statements in General

I am going to assume that since you picked up this book, you are interested in finding out more about financial stuff. Many people dread this topic, but it is very important for every business owner to understand financial matters. How do you make financial decisions if you do not have an understanding of the terms that are being used to describe the options available to you? Questions about pricing and profitability are key to the survival of any business and involve being able to understand financial statements.

This chapter talks about financial statements in general. There are chapters in this book about each of these financial statements. Check out chapters 3 through 5, once you have read this chapter, to get more specific details.

You only need to understand three financial statements—these will tell you the most important things you need to know about your business.

- Balance sheet

- Income statement

- Cash flow statement

The balance sheet shows your assets and liabilities at a particular moment in time. The balance sheet calculates the equity of your business based on some accounting definitions. A business has equity if it has more assets than liabilities. Most businesses exist for the purpose of increasing the shareholder's equity, so it is crucial that you see how that is calculated. As a business owner, one of your goals is to increase the value of your business so you can eventually sell it—the equity of your business is a key concept! Many business owners want to know what their business is worth.

The income statement is the most popular of the basic financial statements—if I can use that terminology. Popular and accounting aren't normally found in the same sentence. The income statement tells you if your business is making money or not. Most people care deeply about that calculation. The income statement compares revenues with expenses and tells you whether you have made a profit or not. If you have not heard this, let me be the one to tell you that as a business owner you want to make money.

Nothing in this book is intended to replace professional advice tailored to your specific situation. You should consult your advisor before making any decisions.

The cash flow statement is not as popular or prepared as often as the other statements, but it has its uses. The cash flow statement can explain to you where your money came from and more importantly where it went!

So you have three financial statements—the balance sheet tells you what you have and what you owe; the income statement tells you if you are making money or not; and the cash flow statements explain where your money came from and where it went. These are all good things to know. There is more to learn of course, as there are some tricks to understanding the way that items are recorded in the accounting records. So now that you know why you care, let's get a little deeper into these statements.

Financial statements always reflect historical amounts. There is no future information on the financial statements. If you see the words forecast, projected, or pro forma, then you know that you are dealing with information that has been made up. No one can reliably predict the future, so don't get too excited about any forecast information. Predictions are just that—when you see the word forecast applied to a financial statement, think about how reliable weather forecasts are.

The actual financial statements that are prepared by professional accountants are historical, that is, they reflect transactions that have already happened. So you should put more faith in financial statements than weather forecasts.

Another very important point is that financial statements reflect transactions. If there is no transaction, then there is nothing recorded on the financial statement. Financial statements are accurate only if all the relevant information is obtained. The financial statements are only as good as the information that was used to prepare them. If you know that some of your transactions have never been given to your accountant, then you should know that your financial statements are not accurate.

There is a chapter in this book about accountant communications, chapter 10, and it explains all about the differences between audits, reviews, and notice to reader communications. They will help you to know what confidence you can place in a particular financial statement depending on what level of assurance an accountant has provided.

Let's look at some of the accounting definitions so we all understand what is being discussed here. We are going to define assets, liabilities, equity, revenues, and expenses. You will find assets, liabilities, and equity on the balance sheet and revenue and expenses on the income statement.

Assets

Let's start with assets although assets are one of the hardest terms to understand. The accounting definition for assets is actually fairly narrow.

An asset is a valuable resource owned by the business. What do we mean by resource? An economic resource is either cash or something that can be converted into cash or something that is expected to be used in future activities that will generate cash inflow to the business.

Some examples will help. An amount owing to the business by a customer is an asset because it will turn into cash when the customer pays it. This is an account receivable. If you are a convenience store, then the milk in the cooler is an asset because it will be sold and you trade the milk for cash. A computer is an asset because you use it in your business to make money. (The definition above talks of generating cash inflow to the business, people who are not accountants simply refer to this as making money.) Cash, accounts receivable, and inventory are typical examples of assets.

Let's work with the definition a little more. The more official definition of an asset is as follows:

- Must be acquired in a transaction

- Must be an economic resource providing future benefits to the entity

- Must be controlled by the entity

- Must be objectively measurable

Okay, let's use an example to show how this works. Many annual reports have a line in the report that says something like "Our employees are our most important assets." This might make sense to human resource professionals, but a professional accountant would be likely to point out that you will never see the category "employee" on a balance sheet. Employees do not meet the criteria for being an asset by accounting standards. Let's look at the definitions. Is an employee acquired in a transaction? Well, slavery is illegal in Canada, so for Canadian accounting purposes employees cannot be assets. How about "must be an economic resource"? Can we turn an employee into cash? Can we determine the cost of the employee? None of those things will work for accounting purposes. Now, this just means that employees are not assets for accounting purposes. You can still refer to something as an asset, but know that you are not talking about accounting assets.

When I am teaching a course, at this point someone usually says but what about athletes? Is it not true that Sydney Crosby is owned by the Pittsburgh Penguins of the National Hockey League? The answer to that question is no. Sydney's contract to play hockey is owned by the Penguins; Syd himself is not owned. If he chooses to cease playing hockey then Pittsburgh will no longer be bossing him around.

Assets on the balance sheet must meet the above definition. This can cause some trouble. For example, software development people are often working on a project that they think is a new asset. Accountants do not agree; they need proof that it is a viable product. Until you actually have a purchase order for a new product, it is not considered to be an economic resource providing future benefits. So accountants fight with software designers about showing all their development work as assets on the balance sheet. The software developers feel that they have created an asset and the accountants feel that there is not yet any proof that an asset has been created. Think about how exciting that meeting would be—two different sorts of geeks engaged in combat!

Assets are the hardest category to understand, so we started with that since you are more likely to be rested at the beginning of the chapter than at the end.

Liabilities

Liabilities are a piece of cake to understand after you have spent time thinking about assets. Liabilities are amounts that you owe to others—a claim on the resources of the business.

Here's the more stuck-up version.

A liability is an obligation to transfer assets or provide services to outside parties arising from events that have already happened.

That definition is a bit shorter than the one for assets.

Examples of liabilities include mortgages, bank loans, accounts payable, and deferred revenue. A mortgage is the obligation to make monthly payments repaying the debt on a house for as many years as it takes to pay it off! Bank loans are for things like buying a car or a big piece of equipment. Accounts payable is the term for when your business owes money to your suppliers. There are other chapters in this book about how to finance your business and how to use debt.

A liability that is occasionally overlooked is deferred revenue. You have deferred or unearned revenue on your books when you have received payment for work that you have not yet completed. Perhaps you asked for payment up front. This amount is treated as a liability because you have the obligation to either do the work or give them back the money. You will record the amount as revenue once you have done the work. Gift certificates are another example of deferred revenue. If your business issues gift cards or certificates, then you have the money from your customers before you give them the product. Gift certificate liability is carried on the balance sheet as a liability until the card holder shows up and gets their products.

Any time your business owes money to someone else, there should be a liability shown on your balance sheet.

Equity

Equity is shown on the bottom of a balance sheet. You see equity when the business has more assets than liabilities. If a business has more liabilities than assets, the name for that is deficiency or deficit. As a business owner, you would prefer to have equity. You would prefer to **have** more than you owe.

If your business is incorporated, then there will be a category for common shares or preferred shares on your balance sheet. The amount that shows in that section of the balance sheet is the amount that you as an individual paid for the shares that were issued by your corporation. The people who own a corporation are known as shareholders and they have paid for the shares by giving the corporation their money. A business only gets the money that a shareholder pays for a share the first time it is sold, because it is only then that the share is sold by the company. Every other sale after that original transaction is a sale that is made by a shareholder to another shareholder.

In small businesses, you will typically see the common share amount as something like $100. This is the amount that was paid by the original shareholders for the shares. In public companies the share capital is much larger.

There is also a line for retained earnings on the financial statements. This line proves that the balance sheet balances. The line for retained earnings contains the net effect of all of the transactions that have ever been made for this corporation. The idea of retained earnings is much what it sounds like—earnings retained by the business. Say it slowly, **earnings retained by the business**. So if the business has had more revenues than expenses over its lifetime, then there is a positive amount known as retained earnings. If the corporation has had more expenses then revenue in its lifetime, then the amount that is shown in this section of the balance sheet is called a deficit.

Let's move on to the income statement. I think you will find that the definitions of revenue and expenses are a little easier to handle.

Revenue

Revenue is the amount that you have charged your customers for your product or service. If you sell chocolate bars for $2, then $2 is your revenue. Revenue is the word we use that also includes the terms sales or fees. We generally refer to sales when we sell a product and fees when we sell a service. It is revenue even if you have not received the money.

Expenses

Remember the discussion about assets? Well, an expense is anything that you have to pay for that does not meet the criteria of being an asset. If you bought something and it is not a fixed asset, an inventory item, or a prepaid, then you have an expense. There is much more information on the differences between assets and expenses in chapter 9.

Cash Flow

When an organization refers to cash flow it can be either positive cash flow which means the organization is receiving more cash than it is sending out, or negative cash flow which means more cash is leaving the organization than is coming in. Cash flow is different than profits. A profit is earned when there is more revenue than expenses. Revenue is not always received as soon as it is billed and expenses are not always paid as soon as they are incurred.

Conclusion

This chapter set the stage for a more detailed understanding of financial statements. We have talked about why you care about financial statements, what they are trying to tell you, and some key definitions. There are other chapters in this book about each statement as well as more detail in areas of expenses, leverage, and revenue recognition. You have much to look forward to.

Notes and Doodles

Chapter 2. Organization Type

How you have organized your business plays a role in how you manage your business and how the profits of your business are taxed. It also determines some of the accounting policies that must be followed. A corporation has to pay more attention to the financial rules than a proprietor does. In fact, the kind of organization you are involved with can also determine the financial statements that have to be prepared and what they are called.

Check out chapter 7—how generally accepted accounting principles (GAAP) have multiplied.

The most common organization types are proprietorship, partnership, corporation, society, or charity. We will talk about each of these possibilities in turn.

Businesses

The simplest form of business is known as a sole proprietorship and is so simple that you may not have even registered the business with anyone. A proprietorship rarely has a balance sheet or a cash flow statement. Most proprietors are running a one-person business that does not have employees. If you have a paper route or you do a little work for someone who does not give you a T4 then you are operating a proprietorship. The proprietorship is the first step in most business ventures. Most people do not incorporate right away—they wait until they are sure that their business idea is going to work for them.

A successful business often starts as a proprietorship and then becomes incorporated as they make more money. Eventually the business may involve holding companies and family trusts. The proprietorship is the first step. There is no cost to carrying on a business as a proprietor unless you decide to register your name with the joint stock registry in your province. You don't need to see a lawyer to start a business as a proprietorship, which might be a benefit depending on how you feel about your lawyer.

In a proprietorship, there is no legal separation between the proprietor and the business. So the proprietor is personally liable for everything that happens with that business. This also means the business income will be included on the tax return of the proprietor, resulting in personal income tax being paid on the profits of the proprietorship.

Once the proprietorship is successful, the amount of personal tax being paid on the profits can be onerous. This is usually why people incorporate their businesses. They want to avoid the higher personal income tax on their business profits and pay only the corporate tax rate. For a detailed discussion on the benefits of incorporation, you should read my book *Ten Tax Traps to Avoid.*

The financial statements of a proprietorship only include the business assets of the proprietorship and do not include any personal assets. The income taxes owed on the business income will not be shown on the income statement of the proprietorship. If you are looking at the financial statements of a proprietorship before buying that business, remember that you cannot buy the shares of this business because there are no shares. The financial statements of a proprietorship are usually incomplete. Very few proprietors bother with a balance sheet and cash flow statement.

The difference between a proprietorship and a partnership is only the number of owners involved. If there is more than one person in a business and that business is not incorporated, then the business is a partnership. Partnership income is also taxed on the personal income tax returns of the partners. If there are two partners and they agree to share the profits equally then each partner would declare 50 percent of the profits on their personal tax return each year. The partnership would prepare an income statement and both partners would file the same income statement with their return. (In case you care, the form you need is T2125.) In addition, in partnerships, each partner is liable for all the business decisions, even those made by the other partner.

The next step for a business that is enjoying financial success is to become incorporated. This means that you have visited a lawyer's office and have created a corporation—a separate legal entity from yourself. Like giving birth without the screaming. When you incorporate your business, this corporation has to file corporate income tax returns, which means that it must prepare both an income statement and a balance sheet. Corporations also must have an accounting system. Generally if a business is incorporated, it will have official financial statements and better information for people to look at. Corporations have to file much more detail with their corporate income tax returns than individuals do. A corporation must file a balance sheet and an income statement and must also show Canada Revenue Agency (CRA) the notes to the financial statements. See chapter 6 on financial statement notes.

Financial literacy is much more important for the owners of an incorporated business than for proprietors. There is simply a lot more emphasis on financial statements.

Society

If you are involved with a non-profit organization (NPO), then you need to understand the financial statements. You are probably involved with a group of people and there will be many meetings. Financial statements will be passed around at these meetings. Because the society is an incorporated entity, the society will need to have a balance sheet, an income statement, and maybe a cash flow statement. The main issue with a society is that you are not dealing with your own money. You are accountable for managing the funds raised from donors or funding agencies. A society is not a taxable entity, but will still have to file information with CRA. The liability for the activities of a society is with the directors. If you are a director, then you have some personal liability if things go wrong at the society. If you are serving as a director on a non-profit board, you should read my book on governance *Basic Board Governance— Governance You Do Not Have to Be a Director to Understand.*

A prudent board member (director) will make sure that the organization has errors and omissions insurance as well as lots of other types of insurance. The problem with being a board member is that you are the one who is liable. So you want to be very careful about understanding the financial situation of the society that you are responsible for.

Charity

A charity is the only form of organization that can issue a charitable donation receipt. A charitable donation receipt is the best kind of donation receipt because it is the only kind of receipt that meets the criteria for being deducted from a personal income tax return. There is additional scrutiny that comes with being a charity. A charity must prepare a balance sheet, an income statement, and notes to the financial statements. A separate charity return must be filed within six months of the year-end of the charity. Failure to file the return on time will lead to the charity losing its charitable status—so you want to understand the process of getting those statements and returns done on time.

Conclusion

Depending on what sort of entity you are involved with, you may need a more or less detailed understanding of financial management topics. The proprietorship is the simplest form of business and the corporation will be the most complex. Recognize that charities and societies are also corporations and that if you are associated with them you need to understand lots of financial stuff.

Chapter 3. Balance Sheet

What are you going to do if someone hands you a balance sheet? Why do you care about a balance sheet? Did you read chapter 1?

To begin with, don't panic, the numbers can be explained. Keep this in mind—the primary purpose of a balance sheet is to show you what the organization has and what it owes. Now that is a simplification, but once you understand some of the weird things about a balance sheet you will have a better idea of stuck-up stuff like solvency and liquidity. And even equity. A balance sheet shows you the equity of a business, within reason. There are a bunch of accounting rules that you will need to understand, a little bit anyway, in order to understand what the balance sheet can tell you and what it cannot.

First of all, balance sheets are historical documents, which means that the balance sheet shows you the financial status at a time that has already passed. If financial statements are talking about the future, they have words such as projected, forecast, or budgeted in their title. That is how you know you are dealing with predictions of the future. If the document just says balance sheet, then it is talking about a time in the past. You should note the date on the balance sheet because anything that has happened since then is not going to be reflected on the statement.

Secondly, all accounting systems record transactions, transactions that have some proof, such as invoices, cheque copies, deposit books, receipts—you get the idea. So, if there has not been a transaction, then nothing is recorded in the books. Seems obvious but this will be more interesting to you once you understand the difference between cost and value.

Do you want to know how much your business has and how much it owes?

The balance sheet tells you what your business owns and owes at a certain point in time. It is composed of assets—what you own—and liabilities, what you owe. The difference between the assets and liabilities is known as the equity in the business. If you were to sell all of your assets and then pay off all of your liabilities, the money you would have left over is called your equity.

You have heard of the term "the equity in your home." This is the difference between what you could sell your house for and the mortgage balance. You also have equity in your business, which is the difference between what the business owns and what the business owes.

Table 1. Example of a balance sheet

Bob's Big Business BALANCE SHEET	THIS YEAR	LAST YEAR
ASSETS		
CURRENT		
Cash	$57,000	$58,000
Accounts receivable	209,811	207,000
Inventory	47,000	51,000
	313,811	316,000
Fixed assets (Note 1)	158,000	162,000
Intangible assets	12,000	12,000
	$483,811	$490,000
LIABILITIES		
CURRENT		
Accounts payable	$89,103	$85,000
Demand loan	52,708	41,000
HST payable	6,000	6,000
Current portion of long-term debt	25,000	24,000
	172,811	156,000
LONG-TERM		
Mortgage	300,000	325,000
	472,811	481,000
EQUITY		
Capital stock	1,000	1,000
Retained earnings	10,000	8,000
	11,000	9,000
	$483,811	$490,000

Table 1 is an example of a balance sheet. This is called a balance sheet because there are two numbers on the statement that must be the same, in other words they must balance. In this case, they are the two $483,811 amounts for the column headed "this year" and the two $490,000 amounts for the column headed "last year," shown in table 1 with a double underline. (Double underlining is very important in the exciting world of accounting. The number that has been "double underlined" is the total of every number above it. Now you know one of our accounting secrets.) Neither of the double underlined totals are named; you are expected to know what the numbers represent.

The balance sheet also includes subtotals. None of the subtotals are named either, and again, as accountants we get paid to tell you what they mean. In table 1 the $313,811 in "this year" is the subtotal of current assets. (These are items that are already cash or should turn into cash within a year, more on this later.) Further down the balance sheet is another subtotal of $172,811. This is the total of current liabilities. Again, these liabilities should be paid within the year.

Balance sheets must balance—there are no exceptions. If the statement you are looking at does not balance, then you should immediately stop looking at it, because it is wrong and you don't want wrong things getting into your head! Of course, it could still be wrong and balance but that is a separate issue. You will also see in table 1 that assets are shown first and are totalled. The rest of the statement must then add up to the total of the assets, which in table 1 is $483,811. One way to look at this is to think about what you have or own—meaning assets—as financed either by debt or the company's retained earnings. (The company's retained earnings are also known as equity.) This statement shows there is $472,811 in liabilities and $11,000 in equity. This means more of the assets are financed with debt than with equity. More on this later, we have a lot of balance sheet stuff to discuss and it will all make sense to you by the end of the book.

Why does a balance sheet balance? Well, it contains, in summarized form, all of the transactions that have ever occurred to the business. How can that be! The balance sheet only shows the assets and liabilities at the moment in time that the balance sheet was prepared but the retained earnings number in the equity section is the sum total of all the revenues and all the expenses that have been incurred by the business since it was born. The income statement summarizes this revenue and expense activity by year but the total of all the years is shown in the retained earnings. We will talk more about income statements as well as retained earnings. Retained earnings is one of the more difficult concepts to grasp so don't give up yet.

What else does the balance sheet tell us? Let's take a more detailed look at what each category means.

Current Assets

The first category on the balance sheet is something known as current assets. Current generally means that the asset can be turned into cash within one year. When we use the term "turn into cash," we mean the assets such as accounts receivable and inventory will be changed into cash. How is this magical process achieved you ask? Accounts receivables will be collected. We no longer have the receivable but we do have the money, so we use the slang term "turn into cash" to explain. Inventory will be sold and the money we charge for the inventory will be collected and this turns the inventory into cash.

The first asset we will discuss is cash. It gets to be first because it is already cash! The assets are presented on the balance sheet in their order of liquidity. Doesn't that sound fancy? What it means is that we list them on the page in the order in which they should turn into cash, so since cash is already cash, it gets to go first! All of the assets that are shown in the current asset category on the balance sheet will eventually turn into cash. They are known as monetary assets for this reason.

If you did not read chapter 1 on financial statements in general yet, you might want to return to that chapter. That is the chapter that has the definitions of assets, liabilities, etc., and will help you understand the balance sheet better.

Cash

What do we mean when we say cash and what is the difference between cash and bank? Technically, cash means there is currency at the business premises, such as a float in a cash register or a pile of $20 bills in a safe. Bank means there is money on deposit in a bank account. However, cash and bank are two words that tend to be used interchangeably by accountants, and I will use cash to mean both in this book.

So let's return to our example in table 1. We know this business has money in the bank, which is always nice. Note that although the word used is cash, we would want to see a note to the financial statements explaining what makes up this number.

In table 1, the business has less cash than it has accounts payable. This means that in order to pay their suppliers the company has to collect its accounts receivable and sell some inventory. As a general rule, most people are happier with their businesses when they have enough money to pay their bills. Comparing the money in the bank with the amount of money that is owed to suppliers is a good comparison to make.

There are other terms used when we speak of cash. You see the words cash and cash equivalents on financial statements for large organizations. What sort of investment is considered to be a cash equivalent? Such items include guaranteed investment certificates, term deposits, money market funds, and certificates of deposit.

Table 2. Example of a cash note

	THIS YEAR	LAST YEAR
Cash on hand and balances with bank	$5,000	$2,000
Cheques issued and outstanding	12,000	11,000
Money market funds	40,000	45,000
	$57,000	$58,000

Cash and cash equivalents consist of cash on deposit, cheques issued and outstanding, and investments in money market instruments.

Accounts Receivable

Accounts receivable arise when the business makes a sale but has not yet been paid. If you have a choice, you should get paid by your customers as soon as you render the service or deliver the product. (See chapter 14 on working capital management for a discussion of ways to collect accounts receivable.)

Accounts receivable are shown after cash on the balance sheet because you typically have to wait for your accounts receivable to turn into cash. We financial types consider accounts receivable to be an asset that is not as useful as cash. Receivables are not as good as cash because you can't pay your bills with receivables; you need the actual currency on deposit. The accounting system will be able to generate an accounts receivable listing that should agree to the number shown on the balance sheet. This listing is very useful because it shows you how old the accounts receivable are and if any of them should be written off.

Table 3. Example of an accounts receivable aged analysis

Bob's Big Business
ACCOUNTS RECEIVABLE AGED ANALYSIS

Name	Total	Current	31–60	61–90	91+
Askew Shopping Centre	$11,912.31	$11,912.31	$0.00	$0.00	$0.00
Belvedere Nursing Home	13,546.20	13,546.20	0.00	0.00	0.00
Construction Concrete Corp.	2,676.72	0.00	0.00	2,676.72	0.00
DAB Collision Ltd.	159.60	0.00	0.00	0.00	159.60
District of Slocan	63,470.58	63,470.58	0.00	0.00	0.00
Gigi's Pasta & Pizza	2,525.20	0.00	2,525.20	0.00	0.00
Lowland Brewery Inc.	2,996.00	0.00	2,996.00	0.00	0.00
New Look Exteriors	23,518.60	23,518.60	0.00	0.00	0.00
Boxborough Paints	8,267.65	8,267.65	0.00	0.00	0.00
South Flats Drainage Board	18,707.62	18,707.62	0.00	0.00	0.00
Travel Ways Inc.	35,732.50	17,128.50	18,069.00	0.00	535.00
Village Realty	15,702.09	15,702.09	0.00	0.00	0.00
West Coast Development	10,596.00	10,596.00	0.00	0.00	0.00
Total outstanding	**$209,811.07**	**$182,849.55**	**$23,590.20**	**$2,676.72**	**$694.60**

Accounts receivable are assets until they are no longer collectible. If a customer has owed the business money for more than three months, it is likely that the bank will not recognize it as an asset. This is because the bank thinks you will not get paid. The bank will not include the older receivables in the total that it considers to be security on the business's line of credit. In table 3 the $694.60 column would be considered for a write-off.

There are certainly times when a customer owes you money for more than ninety days and still pays it. If you believe that you will be paid, then you can leave the amount on your balance sheet as an asset. If you decide that you are not going to get paid, then you actually will remove the receivable from the balance sheet. This is known as "writing it off" and the amount of the receivable moves from the balance sheet where it was enjoying itself as an asset to the income statement where it becomes an expense. There is only one benefit to this move. Since you did not collect the GST/HST and you have included the GST/HST in your returns to CRA, you are now allowed to subtract it.

Otherwise, you are not all that excited about a bad debt because this means that you have been ripped off by a customer and have wasted your time and not gotten paid. This is why, in the scheme of things, accounts receivable are not as good as cash. You always run the risk of not getting your money when you agree to wait for it.

Prepaid Expenses (Prepaids)

Hold on now—Why would any item with expense in its name be on a balance sheet? It's because the term prepaid expense is different than the term advertising expense, for example. A prepaid expense is an amount that has been paid, but the item has not yet been used. That means that it is considered an asset for accounting purposes.

Let's try an example. Some businesses pay their annual insurance bill at the beginning of the year. So let's say that you have an insurance bill of $1200 for your business for the year. If you pay it all at once in January, your bookkeeper is going to put that entire $1200 amount in an account called prepaid insurance. As each month goes by, he or she will take $100 out of prepaid insurance on the balance sheet and put it in insurance expense on the income statement, effectively turning an asset into an expense. Thus, as each month goes by, the business "uses up" $100 of the insurance and that amount stops being prepaid and is an actual expense. The theory is that you would be able to get a refund of the portion of that insurance that you have not used, if in fact you decided to cancel your insurance policy. So, because you could get a refund, the prepaid expense is considered to be an asset.

There are other prepaid expenses. Anything you pay for ahead of time is a prepaid—membership fees, property taxes, subscriptions, along with those airfares you have paid for trips that are yet to happen.

A plane ticket for a trip in March should be expensed in the month of March. If it was paid for in February we show it as prepaid expense in February. When March comes along, we are able to move the asset from prepaids and put it where it belongs in expenses and in the correct month. So when you see prepaid expenses on the balance sheet don't get too excited. Prepaids are more of an accounting asset than an asset that makes sense to regular people. For example, in our original example, that $1200 could be put in expenses in January rather than setting it up in prepaids and making eleven more entries.

I am happy to agree that a prepaid expense is not a very **good** asset.

How accurate do you expect your monthly financial statements to be? Do you pore over these monthly numbers and make business decisions based on the information you glean from the reports? If so, then you want the monthly statements to be very accurate. If not, maybe you should expense the insurance in January and not make the extra eleven entries. Some people make the monthly entries from prepaid expense to insurance because they like bookkeeping. You should attempt to balance the time you spend on your bookkeeping with the value of the information you are receiving.

Inventory

Inventory represents the products your business has on hand that you are hoping to sell to your customers. We are going to discuss inventory in more detail in chapter 14 on working capital management.

The amount of inventory that this business has on hand is tying up its funds and is keeping the company from having that money in the bank. The business has bought inventory but has not sold it. Until such time as inventory is sold, it is an asset.

Possibly a large amount of inventory was purchased because there was a "great deal" if larger quantities were purchased. This business decision should consider a number of variables. A business has to have inventory in order to sell it, but too much inventory is a drain on your cash flow.

We will talk about inventory a lot because the strategies around dealing with inventory are very interesting. How do you decide what product to buy in order to have products to sell to your customers? There is a bit of crystal ball gazing involved here. How can you predict what customers are going to want to buy? When a business guesses wrong, it can end up with inventory that it will be unable to sell at all. In any event, inventory is not as good an asset as cash as it is two steps away from being cash. First you have to sell the inventory and then you have to collect the money. So receivables are shown ahead of inventory on the balance sheet because the receivable should turn into cash in a month or so but inventory first needs to be sold and then the money collected.

If the inventory cannot be sold, then that inventory is no longer considered to be an asset and must leave its cushy life on the balance sheet and become a part of the cost of goods sold category on the income statement. There are times when it is easy to decide that inventory can no longer be sold, such as three-week-old milk or rotting vegetables. However, if the items your business sells are not perishable, then you have a harder choice to make. Are the items obsolete? Are you still stocking 5 1/4 inch floppy disks? If so you will not have many sales! Not every example is this clear. Accountants spend much time discussing the sales prospects of various inventory items with the sales department. Sales people are naturally optimistic and accounting types tend to be more sceptical, so these are riveting discussions. Perhaps you could ask to be invited next time.

So that is pretty much it for the current asset category. If you see any other items listed in the current asset section then the decision has been made that the item is going to turn into cash within a year of the date on the balance sheet. These other items could be taxes receivable or short-term loans to related parties.

Fixed Assets

The business referenced in table 1 also has fixed assets on the balance sheet. We sometimes see different terminology for fixed assets—they are also known as capital assets, or maybe just property and equipment. If you see these categories on the balance sheet, it means the organization has purchased items such as land, buildings, computers, office equipment, and/or vehicles. Fixed assets are shown separately from current assets because it is not expected the fixed assets will be turned into cash within a year. In fact, fixed assets are not for sale; they are for use in the business.

The number showing on the balance sheet is the "net book value" of these items, not what the assets might be sold for. In other words, it is the amortized cost, not the value of the assets. (See chapter 6 for a discussion of the cost principle to see why values are not always shown on a balance sheet.)

There should be a note attached to the financial statements that will show the categories of the fixed assets, their original purchase price, and how much has been written off as depreciation (or amortization). Accumulated depreciation (or amortization) is the term for the amount that has been written off over the life of the assets to date. Table 4 provides an example of this type of note.

Table 4. Example of a fixed asset note to the financial statements

Bob's Big Business
NOTES TO THE FINANCIAL STATEMENTS
FIXED ASSETS NOTE

	THIS YEAR COST	THIS YEAR ACCUMULATED DEPRECIATION	THIS YEAR NET BOOK VALUE	LAST YEAR NET BOOK VALUE
Land	$25,000	$0	$25,000	$25,000
Building	150,000	23,000	127,000	130,000
Tools	10,000	9,000	1,000	1,200
Vehicle	25,000	20,000	5,000	5,800
	$210,000	$52,000	$158,000	$162,000

Fixed assets are on the balance sheet because they are the type of asset that gets used up over time, not immediately. We use vehicles in our businesses and typically the vehicles last more than one year. We can't just put the vehicle on the income statement and call it an expense. Most businesses have a policy of some type that sets a limit for purchases of equipment that will be expensed compared to equipment purchases that will be capitalized. So let me explain that—if you capitalize a piece of equipment it means that you put that piece of equipment on the balance sheet. If you expense a piece of equipment then you put it on the income statement. We have an entire chapter (chapter 9) devoted to the discussion about whether a purchase is an expense or an asset. This is an important decision because anything that is placed on the balance sheet adds to the equity of a business and anything that is placed on the income statement will reduce the equity of the business so we need to have rules. Most places will set a limit of $500 or so ,to decide if an asset belongs on the balance sheet or income statement and the higher dollar value items will be placed on the balance sheet.

Once an asset is capitalized, (which means put on the balance sheet) it will begin to be depreciated. This is to recognize, for accounting purposes, that we are using an asset in our business. Fixed assets are different from inventory because inventory is for sale and fixed assets are being used in the business. But we do want to acknowledge on the financial statements that we are using assets to run the business. So accountants developed this arbitrary method called depreciation, sometimes also called amortization. Either word is used.

To depreciate an asset, we take a percentage of the cost of the asset and apply it to the asset and call it depreciation. So if we had a $10,000 asset and we were depreciating it at 20 percent we would depreciate $2000 a year. Effectively, we reduce the cost of the asset by $2,000 on the balance sheet and record a depreciation expense on the income statement. We will talk more about depreciation in chapter 9 because it is an interesting expense.

Depreciation is an expense without writing a cheque. All we are doing is allocating cost—we are arbitrarily moving value from the balance sheet. There is much to be discussed here because we tend to think about fixed assets in terms of value; we think that because the asset is getting used up that we are reducing its value. But we also depreciate buildings and it is rare for a building to decrease in value. So remember that **the depreciation of an asset is done to recognize its use—not to try and show its value.** We will talk more about whether assets are recorded at cost or value on the financial statements and how the choice of accounting policies affect that decision.

Back to our note (table 4). Once you read the note, you will know what kind of assets have been purchased by the business. In the case above, you will see that the tools and vehicle are probably fairly old as they have been almost fully depreciated. This makes sense when you think about it because the longer you have owned an asset the more you have depreciated it and the lower its cost will be on the balance sheet. The land is shown at its original cost and has not been depreciated as we do not depreciate land; we assume that it never gets used up. The building is being depreciated despite the fact that it is likely increasing in value. Remember that the cost on the balance sheet does not reflect the value of the assets.

Long-term Assets

We have talked about current assets, which are those assets that will turn into cash within a year. But there are other monetary assets that are just not current. What if you have an account receivable from a client who is paying you but is not going to be able to pay you all that they owe within a year? The receivable is still an asset but it will not meet the criteria of a current asset. A current asset turns into cash within one year.

We also might have loans receivable from other companies we do business with that are not going to be repaid in a year. So any asset that is going to be turned into cash in a time period longer than a year is shown in the long-term section of the balance sheet.

Long-term versus Current Assets

What is the big deal with whether an asset is current or long-term? There are a number of ratios that are calculated comparing current assets to current liabilities. Some bank loans have a requirement that a company that borrows money from them must keep their ratios at a certain level. Typically the company must have at least as many current assets as it has current liabilities so the classification of an asset as being a current asset is important to these ratios. See chapter 11 for more on ratios.

Intangible Assets

There are assets that do not have a physical presence, such as goodwill, franchises, patents, and copyrights. These assets are often shown separately from the fixed assets on the balance sheet. We will take a look at each category.

Goodwill

If you see goodwill on the balance sheet then the business has actually purchased this goodwill from another business. Remember the discussion in chapter 1 about how accountants record assets. We don't record something unless there is a transaction. So there are many companies who have goodwill, but most of those companies would not have it showing on their statements because there is no transaction for it.

My favourite example of goodwill not being on a balance sheet relates to my accounting practice. If you were to visit my office, you would see desks, computers, and filing cabinets. The value of these assets would not be significant. If you were to venture down the hallway from my office to the other side of the building and set up an office containing desks, computers, and filing cabinets, you would have an office that would look very much like mine. What is the difference between rooms full of desks and computers and an accounting practice? Well, the big difference is that I have a bunch of clients and the other office does not. So it is fair to say that the biggest asset of my accounting practice is my client list. I have not paid for that list though, so it is not on my balance sheet.

This seems weird to all of us—the biggest asset of an organization is not on the financial statement that shows you all of the assets. This is one of the main reasons why we have to understand the accounting rules. Balance sheets are not about value (except if your company follows IFRS, see chapter 7). Balance sheets generally show the cost of assets, not their value. All bookkeeping is based on transactions. If I purchased a client list, then this asset would be on my balance sheet.

When you are looking at financial statements for the purposes of valuing a business, remember that you need more information than what you see on the financial statements. The balance sheet will not include some assets that you would be willing to pay for such as websites, phone numbers, intellectual property, and logos.

Franchises

If you own a franchise, then you would have paid some money for this franchise. The amount of this payment is recorded on your balance sheet. Any increase in the value of this franchise since you bought it is not going to be recorded on the balance sheet. Same rules as for goodwill that we discussed above. You record transactions, not any increase in value that is not proven. We financial types feel that an increase in value should not be recorded without evidence, and the best evidence is someone actually paying for it.

Copyrights

A copyright is much what it sounds like. You have obtained the legal right to keep other people from using your work for their profit. Copyright refers to written documents and the term of the copyright is for a period of time ending fifty years after the author's death. You can see the cost of a copyright on a balance sheet. The cost to register the copyright of a book is $25 a title. This is not a significant asset on the books of the business. However, keep in mind that the value of holding the right to reproduce a work could be very significant.

Patents

If you have been reading along, you probably know what I am going to say about patents. They are recorded on the books of a business at the price that the patent lawyers and the patent office charge you to register the patent. However the patent could be worth a great deal more money than that—or of course the patent could be for a totally worthless process that is not even worth the price of paying the patent lawyer.

Current Liabilities

The business identified in table 1 has four current liabilities listed on its balance sheet. This means it has four debts that must be paid within the coming year. That is what "current" means. Most times however the debt has to be paid in thirty or sixty days. The one-year criterion is the cut off date for when the debt would have to be moved to the long-term liability section.

Remember, we care about the characterization of assets and liabilities into current and long-term so that we can analyze things like solvency, liquidity, and working capital management. We have fabulous information about these topics in this book, so if you can't wait, check out the relevant chapters now.

Line of Credit or Bank Overdraft

We talked about cash when we were discussing current assets. If

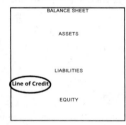

your organization does not, in fact, have money in the bank, then it does not have a current asset. If your bank account is overdrawn and you are using your overdraft or a line of credit, then you have a current liability. That is, you will pay back this money within a year, or the lender has the right to request repayment within the year.

A business could have cash on the balance sheet in the asset section and a line of credit showing on the current liability section. Some banks require two separate accounts—one for your line of credit and one for your actual bank balance. The bank wants you to have money in the bank account all of the time and you could end up borrowing money on your line to make sure there is always money in that account. Other banks combine the two and simply allow you to use your overdraft when you have written cheques for more money than is in the bank.

I am of a fan of having one bank account with an allowable overdraft rather than maintaining two separate accounts. The banks like the idea of two accounts because in that way there may be times when they can charge you interest on your line for part of the balance in your other account. With the one account you are only paying interest on the exact amount that you are borrowing.

Accounts Payable

The accounts payable balance represents amounts owing to suppliers for items that the business has purchased such as inventory or expenses. The suppliers typically want their money in thirty to sixty days. There should be list of accounts payable prepared by the accounting system which agrees to the amount that is shown on the balance sheet. This listing is called an accounts payable summary and provides the reader of the financial statements with the details about whom the business owes and for how long.

Table 5. Example of an accounts payable aged analysis

Bob's Big Business ACCOUNTS PAYABLE AGED ANALYSIS					
Name	Total	Current	31–60	61–90	91+
Abercrombie Hardware Inc.	$37,985.00	$37, 985.00	$0.00	$0.00	$0.00
ACME Novelty Ltd.	(100.00)	0.00	0.00	(100.00)	0.00
Cheshire Development	597.24	0.00	0.00	0.00	597.24
Harry's Lumber	30,308.20	7,002.62	20,983.24	0.00	2,322.34
Heisman Construction	343.10	0.00	0.00	0.00	343.10
Lexigton Drywall Inc.	19,969.42	6,113.82	7,756.56	6,099.04	0.00
Total outstanding	$89,102.96	$51,101.44	$28,739.80	$5,999.04	$3,262.68

HST Payable

The HST payable is the Harmonized Sales Tax that the business has collected from its customers and is shown after subtracting the HST the business has paid on its purchases. The fact that the HST is shown in the current liability section means the business has collected more HST on its sales than it has paid out for expenses. This should be the goal of all businesses—to charge more than they pay out—I hope I am not the first person to say this to you.

If the HST is shown in the current asset section, it means the business is getting a refund of HST because it has paid out more HST than it has collected. Generally a business would prefer to pay in HST because this means that it has more revenue than expenses as I have said, but there are times when a business will have a refund because the business has purchased lots of equipment or inventory.

Some business such as fishers and farmers are always getting HST refunds because although they do not charge HST, they are eligible for refunds of any HST they pay for business expenses. Some businesses will not have any HST showing on the balance sheet because they neither collect HST nor do they get a refund. Medical practices and daycares are two examples of businesses that are not permitted to participate in the HST system.

Current Portion of Long-term Debt

All loans, mortgages, and even capital leases have a portion that is due within the coming year and a portion that is due later than this year. I bet you can figure out that the part of the loan that is due within the coming year is called the current portion of the long-term debt. This classification is made because it is important to creditors. Anyone who is a creditor of a company wants to know how much they owe over the next year. This is a calculation of solvency or liquidity and often involves the calculation of ratios. See chapter 11 for more information.

Long-term Liabilities

Any liabilities which show up in this section are liabilities that will be paid off in a period of time that is longer than one year. Similar to the classification of current and long-term assets, we have current and long-term liabilities. The portion of a corporation's debt that is shown in long-term liabilities is the portion that is due after the coming year is over. See the chapter on financing (chapter 12) for more information.

If the financial statements are prepared by a professional accountant, then there is likely to be a note to the financial statements giving more details about this debt such as the amount of the payments, interest rate, the security provided, and the interest rate being charged.

Table 6. Example of a long-term liability note

	2031	2030
7.5% first mortgage payable in monthly blended installments of $69,954, due March 15, 2021, secured by land and building with a net book value of $3,550,000.	$3,121,000	$3,637,000
Current portion of long-term debt	838,000	759,000
	$2,283,000	$2,878,000

Mortgage

A mortgage is the type of loan that a business gets to pay for the purchase of a building. This type of liability will be paid over a long period of time. The amount is usually owing to a bank. Mortgages are a cheaper source of financing than term loans and credit cards. Often there is a note to the financial statements that explains the monthly payment amount, the rate of interest when the mortgage will be up for renewal, and how it is secured.

Term Loans

A term loan is a loan that must be repaid over a specified time period. A car loan is a very good example of this. You make payments every month for a number of years and the loan is eventually paid and the car is all yours. This is a common way to finance an asset. The portion of the loan that is due within a year is shown in current liabilities and the rest of the loan is shown here in long-term liabilities.

Capital Lease Obligations

If an organization is leasing equipment with the intention of owning this equipment then the lease is called a capital lease. Because a capital lease is really not different from a loan, the amount of this lease is shown in the long-term debt section. There will be a note explaining the monthly payment, the interest rate, the security, and when the lease ends.

Table 7. Example of a capital lease note

The company has the following obligations under capital leases:	2031	2030
Agreement bearing interest at 17.75% per annum, requiring blended monthly payments of $298 to October 2032 and a final payment of $540 in November 2034, secured by a vehicle with a net book value of $7,004.	$6,849	$7,392
Agreement bearing interest at 14.75% per annum, requiring blended monthly payments of $399 to October 2032 and final payment of $3,348 in November 2033, secured by a vehicle with a net book value of $11,843.	10,913	14,693
	19,350	22,003
Less: Current portion	5,104	6,203
	$14,246	$15,800

Shareholder Loan

A shareholder loan is an amount that was lent by one or all of the shareholders to the corporation. It often has no fixed terms of repayment and will be repaid to the shareholders if and when there is cash flow available. Accountants don't usually show a current portion of shareholder loans as these loans do not usually have terms of repayment.

This might be another area where you feel differently about the numbers than the accounting professionals. Many people feel that lending money to their business should be considered to be equity. Equity will be discussed in the next section. Sometimes a bank lends money to a business partially because the shareholder has also put money in the business. In this case, the bank might ask for a postponement of claim, that is, the shareholder cannot take the shareholder loan out of the business until the bank says it is okay. Repayment is generally only allowed after the bank has gotten their loan repaid. You could be forgiven for thinking the shareholder loan should be equity.

Equity

Equity is the last category on the balance sheet. Equity is made up of the amounts that shareholders have contributed to the corporation by buying shares and the income that has been made in the company and retained by it. If your business is a public company there will also be other categories such as accumulated comprehensive other income. Non-profit organizations (NPOs) will sometimes have a category known as contributed surplus.

Capital Stock (a.k.a. Common Shares)

What is the $1,000 in capital stock in table 1? Capital stock indicates that this business is incorporated. This is the money shareholders paid for their original shares. If you own all of this company then this is the amount you paid when you first set up the company. This money is in the equity section because the company is not going to return it to you. Capital stock is quite different from a shareholder loan. If you give your company money as a shareholder loan then you can have that money back whenever the company can afford to pay it to you. The shareholder loan is recorded in the liability section as it will be repaid at some point. (See chapter 12 for a discussion of equity financing.)

Capital stock, also known as common shares, is money that shareholders have invested. They bought their shares from the corporation and the amount they paid is shown on the balance sheet as common shares. This amount is not repaid to the shareholders by the company unless the company is closed. Shareholders get their money back by selling their shares to other people. When a business owner wants to sell their business, they have the option to sell their shares to someone who wants to buy the corporation. There are huge tax advantages to selling the shares of a small business. (Check out my book *Ten Tax Traps to Avoid* for the gory details.)

The company only gets money when it originally issues the shares or if it sells some more shares. The initial selling of shares is referred to as an initial public offering. If you are a shareholder, then when you sell your shares to someone else you get the money and the company gets nothing.

If you think about the stock market, most of those transactions are between individual shareholders. If you sell your bank shares on the stock market, then some other person buys them. The bank does not participate in this transaction and nothing happens on their balance sheet.

Retained Earnings

The term retained earnings is pretty much what is sounds like—the amount of earnings retained in the business since the business was born. When a business is profitable it earns an income. Earning an income makes the retained earnings increase. When a business pays out a dividend to the shareholders the retained earnings are decreased. So the amount of retained earnings is the amount of income the business has made in its lifetime less what it has paid out to its shareholders.

When a business has retained earnings, it means the business has been profitable in the past. You don't know when in the past, but you do know that overall the business has been profitable in its lifetime

Contributed Surplus

An NPO may be given assets from another NPO such as another charity. These amounts are shown on the balance sheet as assets and the offsetting amount is shown in contributed surplus—because that balance sheet has to keep on balancing.

Some businesses will also show contributed surplus when complicated tax magic has been done to transfer assets into a corporation. Of course, if we transfer assets into a business and there is no offsetting debt, then contributed surplus is created. If you are reviewing a set of financial statements and there is significant contributed surplus, then you should ask about the intricacies of the transactions that created this weirdness on the balance sheet.

Accumulated Other Comprehensive Income (AOCI)

This sounds much like a collection of buzz words and some might argue that it is! If your organization is following IFRS (International Financial Reporting Standards) then you will see this category in the equity section of the balance sheet. Organizations that follow IFRS are required to show some of their assets at their fair values rather than at their cost. It follows that when the corporation changes the numbers on their balance sheet to the fair values then an offsetting entry has to be made somewhere on the balance sheet. If there was no place to show the other side of the fair value entry we would not have a balance sheet anymore and no one should look at an unbalanced sheet. AOCI (see Appendix B) is where we put the other side of the entries that are made to change cost to fair value on the balance sheet. If your organization does not use IFRS then—happy for you—you do not care about this category on the balance sheet.

Table 8. Example of a balance sheet

Bob's Big Business BALANCE SHEET		THIS YEAR	LAST YEAR
ASSETS			
CURRENT			
Cash		$57,000	$58,000
Accounts receivable		209,811	207,000
Inventory		47,000	51,000
		313,811	316,000
Fixed assets (Note 1)		158,000	162,000
Intangible assets		12,000	12,000
		$483,811	$490,000
LIABILITIES			
CURRENT			
Accounts payable		$89,103	$85,000
Demand loan		52,708	41,000
HST payable		6,000	6,000
Current portion of long-term debt		25,000	24,000
		172,811	156,000
LONG-TERM			
Mortgage		300,000	325,000
		472,811	481,000
EQUITY			
Capital stock		1,000	1,000
Retained earnings		10,000	8,000
		11,000	9,000
		$483,811	$490,000

Comparative Numbers

The financial statements usually have a column for the current year and one for the past year, which is called a comparative number. The statements are prepared on a comparative basis to provide you with more information. You can compare each category with the year before and see the trends. If there were more than two years being presented, the most recent numbers are first after the words and the numbers keep getting older as you move to the right. It is, however, not a bad plan to check this by looking at the dates at the top of each column in case a rebel accountant has prepared the statements and has not followed one of the cardinal rules of accounting.

If you are comparing these two columns, a number of questions might come to mind. For example, if you have more accounts receivable this year than last year, it means your sales have gone up, more people are paying on credit, or you have not been as successful in collecting your money. You will be able to determine which one of these answers is the correct one once you have reviewed the income statement as well. However, you can tell from the fact the retained earnings have increased that you made more money this year. What else do you see? Receivables are up, and inventory is down. These are positive trends.

The fixed assets on the balance sheet are a lower number this year than last year. This means nothing new has been purchased and the fixed assets you have are being depreciated. Depreciation will result in fixed assets being a lower amount each year on the balance sheet unless new fixed assets are purchased.

The accounts payable are up and you still owe Canada Revenue Agency (CRA) the same amount. Although the HST amount appears the same, this is not last year's number, as that balance has been paid. If you had not paid the HST from last year, the balance would be much higher and you would have definitely attracted the attention of CRA's collection department. So looking at just the balance sheet, it appears to be good. Equity has increased. Now you can turn your attention to the income statement to get more information on how this happened. Income statements are discussed in the next chapter.

Conclusion

The balance sheet is an important document for any business owner to understand. The balance sheet shows the owners what they have and what they owe and the difference is the amount of equity in the business.

As most business owners want to increase the shareholders equity in the business, this statement is the one they should look at least every month. Keep in mind that, depending on the accounting policies being used, the balance sheet may not reflect the value of the business. Understanding the differences between accounting and real life is key to figuring out how best to manage a business and what your business might have to sell down the road.

Chapter 4. Income Statement

The income statement is the most popular statement because it shows the business owner whether or not the business is profitable, that is, whether or not you are making money. People usually care more about profits than equity, which is why they like the income statement more than the balance sheet.

This statement is often referred to as the P and L, which means profit and loss. We also hear statement of operations, or the statement of revenue and expenses, or the statement of receipts and disbursements. I am sure you get the idea. Every organization has a statement that tells them whether or not they are making money. It is called various things.

Making money means having revenues that exceed your expenses for the time period on the statement. The income statement covers a period of time—a month, a quarter, or a year. It shows your revenues and your expenses for the same time period. The revenues are the amounts you charge your customers for your goods and services. The expenses are all of the things (that are not assets) you need to spend money on in order to make those revenues.

The income statement in table 9 is for a service business. We know this because there is no cost of goods sold. This business is making money with revenues of $70,000 exceeding expenses of $35,200.

Expenses are items you must purchase in order to make money. The item you purchase is an expense unless it qualifies as an asset. We have discussed assets in the chapter on the balance sheet (chapter 3) and also in the introductory chapter (chapter 1) on financial statements, so hopefully you are becoming more comfortable with the accounting definition of an asset. We also have a chapter on just the decision about whether a purchase is an asset or an expense. If you want you can head there right now, it's chapter 9.

A vehicle that you must use for your business is an example of an item you need in order to earn money—it costs more than $500 and hopefully lasts longer than one year. This means it is an asset, not an expense. You will recall from the previous discussion, assets go on the balance sheet and they fall in the category of things you own. Expenses are items used up in a year, such as the monthly rent you pay on your business premises and salaries paid to your employees. Assets add to the equity of your business and expenses reduce it.

There are two ways to make more money—more revenue or fewer expenses. This sounds simplistic, but it is the truth. You can increase revenue by selling more, selling at a higher price, or selling different products. Expenses can be reduced by using less, finding more cost effective or less expensive sources, or using alternative methods. There have been many books written on methods for increasing profitability, but they are all variations on these two themes. (Chapter 15 has a more in depth discussion of this issue.)

Table 9. Example of an income statement

Bob's Big Business
INCOME STATMENT

	THIS YEAR	LAST YEAR
REVENUE		
Fees	$68,000	$50,000
Other revenue	2,000	5,000
	70,000	55,000
EXPENSES		
Wages	24,300	20,000
Rent	8,100	8,000
Depreciation	1,000	1,000
Advertising	800	1,000
Travel	1,000	1,000
	35,200	31,000
NET INCOME BEFORE TAX		
(*Revenue-Expenses*)	34,800	24,000
Provision for income tax	4,800	4,000
NET INCOME AFTER TAX	30,000	20,000
RETAINED EARNINGS at beginning of year	8,000	16,000
	38,000	36,000
Less: Dividends paid in year	28,000	28,000
RETAINED EARNINGS at end of year	$10,000	$8,000

The income statement in table 9 includes dividends. These payments are made to the shareholders of the company—people like you. Some business owners take dividends instead of a salary. This means the net income of the business will be a higher figure than if the owner manager took a salary. In the sample income statement, if the dividends were removed and the $28,000 was added to salaries then the company would have shown $28,000 less net income. There is a very good tax reason why dividends might be chosen over salaries. Overall, the corporation pays less tax on income than individuals. It can make sense to have the company pay tax and then take what is left over as dividends. There is much more involved in making this decision and I have written another book about taxes, so if this decision is of interest to you check out *Ten Tax Traps to Avoid.*

You will see from the income statement in table 9, the equity of the business has decreased from the beginning of the "last year" to the end of the "current year." The opening retained earnings were $16,000 and at the end of that year were only $8,000. The business earned a net income of $20,000 in that year and the shareholders took $28,000 in dividends. This reduced the retained earnings because there were more dividends removed than income earned. This can be a sign of financial trouble as a business cannot continue to pay more money out than is being earned. If this is your business, you want to watch this comparison as you should not be taking more money out of the business than you are making. The choices are either to reduce what you take out of the business or to make more money!

Statement Preparation

For you to really be able to have a good picture of what is happening with your business, it is important that both the balance sheet and the income statement are prepared at the same time. An income statement without a balance sheet is not as useful for your analysis. This is because there is no proof the income statement includes all of the items it should unless it ends with the correct retained earnings figure. The retained earnings figure must match the number you need on the balance sheet in order to balance that statement. You will note that the $10,000 retained earnings figure appears on both the income statement in table 9 (at the end of the year) and the balance sheet in table 1, so it is safe to look at the income statement.

Turn your attention to the top of the statement in table 9 where you will be pleased to see that revenue has increased. Note, however, that the "other revenue" is down. This could easily have been a strategic move to increase the revenue where there are less costs and decrease the other revenue that was not as profitable. However, if you did not decide to reduce your revenue in this area it could be a cause for concern. Were you aware your "other revenue" was down? If not, then you now know something you did not a few minutes ago and you can take steps to see what is going on.

Moving down the page you see wages are up. It's not a surprise in a service business for wages to rise with revenue, as you are selling time. The key, of course, is to make sure revenue is going up faster than costs, including payroll. Everything else looks pretty consistent from an expense point of view.

From the net income after tax line in table 9, the business shows that it made $10,000 more in the current year than in the previous year. This is a positive trend and one you hope continues. However, the retained earnings at the end of the year of the business only went up by $2,000. This is because the dividends last year were $8,000 in excess of the money earned (net income $20,000 and dividends of $28,000 in table 9) and this year the dividends are less than the money earned (net income $30,000 and dividends $28,000). In other words, you had some catching up to do because you took more than you made last year. So the dividends did not increase, even though you made more money. The decision about the amount of dividends paid in the year is a management decision related to where the money is best used or possibly most needed. Occasionally it will also be a bank decision, as the bank will require you to keep a certain amount of equity.

This type of decision is fundamental to financial management. A business owner has to decide where their money is best used— invested in the business or withdrawn from the business and invested elsewhere? Sometimes this decision is based on whether a business owner believes he or she is building a business that can be sold down the road or not. If the business is not likely to be sold, one strategy would be to remove funds and invest in other businesses, real estate, or the market.

Conclusion

We have looked at some of the basics of reviewing financial statements. The following chapters will expand on accounting principles, practices, and communications. Other chapters will also address some of the decisions that affect the financial statements. Appendix A has a checklist for reviewing financial statements.

Chapter 5. Cash Flow Statement

The cash flow statement is usually the third financial statement in any package you receive from your accountant. What this statement tells you is where the business's cash came from and where it went in the year. This is valuable information because it is not apparent from the other financial statements that we have discussed so far. The balance sheet and income statement are prepared on the "accrual" method of accounting, which means these statements include all the transactions of the business, whether or not the cash has changed hands. To be clear, the income statement we looked at in the last chapter includes all the sales made in the period, whether or not the cash has been received from the customer.

The cash flow statement only shows the cash received (not billed) from the customers. The same scenario is true of expenses. The income statement we looked at includes all of the expenses incurred in the year, whether or not they have been paid, and the cash flow statement only includes the expenses paid in cash. Positive cash flow occurs when more money is received by a business than is spent by the business. A business has a positive cash flow from borrowing money, or from collecting its assets such as receivables, or selling its inventory. A business has negative cash flow from paying back debt, purchasing more assets, or increasing the accounts receivable and inventory. The cash flow statement divides the cash flow from the business into three areas: operating; financing; and, investing. The operating activities are always shown first at the top of this financial statement. Generally a business would prefer to see cash flow from operations rather than cash flow from financing.

Operating Activities

The cash flow from operations of the business are those changes in the balances in the current assets' and the current liabilities' sections of the balance sheet. For example, if the accounts receivable increase year over year, then more cash is being tied up in receivables instead of being in the bank. This is a negative cash flow, or a cash outflow. Conversely, if the accounts receivable decrease from one year to the next, this is a positive cash flow because the business will have more cash, as more customers have paid their bills. The same holds true of inventory. If the business is increasing its inventory then it is using cash to do so. If it is decreasing its inventory, then cash is being freed up, with a resulting positive cash flow. If the business is profitable there will generally be a positive cash flow from operations.

Financing Activities

Financing activities are those activities that involve borrowing money and paying it back. Cash flow from financing involves the long-term debt section of the balance sheet. This cash flow is positive when debt is being incurred and negative when debt is being paid off.

If the business is growing, financing cash flow will be positive as more debt will be incurred. Borrowing money is a positive cash flow as it brings funds into the business. Paying back debt is a negative cash flow as cash is leaving the business by being paid to the creditor. If the owners are remunerating themselves by way of dividends rather than salary, then financing activities will probably show as a negative, because dividends are a negative cash flow shown in the financing section of the cash flow statement.

Less common financing activities include when the corporation issues more shares (positive cash flow), or repurchases some of the shares that are outstanding (negative cash flow).

Investing Activities

Investing activities occur when the business buys more fixed assets or sells some of their fixed assets. Remember, fixed assets include buildings, equipment, land, and vehicles. In general, cash flow from investing involves the long-term asset section of the balance sheet. This cash flow is negative when fixed assets are being purchased and positive when fixed assets are being sold. If the business is growing, you would expect this cash flow to be negative because more assets are being purchased.

In a growing business you will see the positive cash flow from borrowing funds offset by the negative cash flow of purchasing fixed assets. A business generally gets the funds they need to grow by borrowing. (A non-profit organization (NPO) gets money by fundraising.) The cash comes in from the bank and goes out to the supplier of the assets the business is purchasing. If the business is not expanding, or does not use many fixed assets, then you should not see a lot of positive cash flow from financing. What you do not want to see is positive cash flow arising from borrowing money to offset negative cash flow caused by the business losing money. In particular, you do not want to see this if there is any chance that you could be personally liable for repaying the financing.

Preparation Methods

There are two methods of preparing the cash flow statement—the direct and the indirect method. It is possible that you do not care about one of these statements. You should figure out which method is in use in your organization and pay attention to that one.

The choice of method only affects the cash flow from operating activities. The direct method shows cash from customers and cash paid to suppliers and employees in the operating section of the cash flow statement. The indirect method shows the increase or decrease in each line on the balance sheet in the current asset and current liability section. The increases in current assets and decreases in current liabilities are negative cash flow. The decreases in current assets and increases in current liabilities are positive cash flow.

Table 10. Example of a statement of cash flow using the direct method

Bob's Big Business STATEMENT OF CASH FLOW DIRECT METHOD		
	THIS YEAR	LAST YEAR
OPERATING ACTIVITIES		
Cash from customers	$765,513	$733,627
Cash paid to suppliers and employees	-700,319	-652,495
	65,194	81,132
FINANCING ACTIVITIES		
Advances from shareholders	137	0
Dividends paid	-20,000	-20,407
Decrease in long-term debt	-31,342	-31,368
	-51,205	-51,775
INVESTING ACTIVITIES		
Fixed asset additions	-35,937	-11,088
Decrease in cash in year	-21,948	18,269
Cash at beginning of year	138,954	120,685
Cash at end of year	$117,006	$138,954

The indirect method is seen more often, and is illustrated in table 11. Because this method shows the increase or decrease in each line on the balance sheet in the current asset and current liability section, it is a longer statement. I personally do not think the indirect method of preparing cash flow statements is as informative as the direct method, but it is the more common approach. Accountants feel that being able to show their clients what happened line by line on the balance sheet is valuable. Some people don't have that level of interest.

Table 11. Example of a statement of cash flow using the indirect method

Bob's Big Business STATEMENT OF CASH FLOW INDIRECT METHOD		
	THIS YEAR	LAST YEAR
OPERATING ACTIVITIES		
Net income	$120,000	$100,000
(Increase) decrease in receivables	-15,000	20,000
Decrease (increase) in inventories	10,000	-25,000
Decrease in payables	-49,806	-13,868
	65,194	81,132
FINANCING ACTIVITIES		
Advances from shareholders	137	0
Dividends paid	-20,000	-20,407
Decrease in long-term debt	-31,342	-31,368
	-51,205	-51,775
INVESTING ACTIVITIES		
Fixed asset additions	-35,937	-11,088
Decrease in cash in year	-21,948	18,269
Cash at beginning of year	138,954	120,685
Cash at end of year	$117,006	$138,954

The cash flow statements shown in table 10 and 11 are exactly the same except for the differences in the reporting of operating cash flow. These statements show us how the business got its cash and what it did with it. The business is operating at a profit and has positive cash flow from operations. The positive cash flow from operations is being used to pay dividends, pay down debt, and buy assets. This business did not incur any new debt in the year and it did buy more assets. The result is that the amount of cash on hand at the end of the year is lower than at the same time last year.

Conclusion

This chapter has talked about the basics of cash flow statements. So now you know all about balance sheets, income statements and cash flow statements. The other chapters in this book expand on this knowledge.

Notes and Doodles

Chapter 6. Generally Accepted Accounting Practices You Need to Know

The term "generally accepted accounting principles" is usually shortened and just called GAAP. It is pronounced "gap," although it should be pronounced "gaaaaap." These principles are established in Canada by CPA Canada, a group formerly known as the Canadian Institute of Chartered Accountants, or CICA. This accounting group is responsible for the creation of a fascinating volume of accounting pronouncements, known as the CPA Canada Handbook. This tome makes good bedtime reading and could be marketed as an insomnia cure.

So why do you care? Well, the Canadian Business Corporation Act, the Securities Act, and the Income Tax Act use the CPA Canada definitions of GAAP from the CPA Canada Handbook. This means the handbook makes the rules for accounting in Canada and you need to know the rules. If your business borrows money, the bank will have you sign an agreement that requires you to maintain certain financial standards, all calculated using GAAP.

In 2010, GAAP was fractured into a number of parts. The details about this change are found in chapter 7. This chapter is about the basics. More specific information is available depending on whether your organization is a business, a non-profit organization (NPO), a public company, or a pension plan.

What follows are a few of the basics of GAAP explained.

Cash or Accrual Method of Accounting

There are two very basic methods for accounting. One is called cash and the other accrual. Either can be used to prepare internal financial statements, but accrual method is normally used for any statements that are going to be presented to outside parties. Farmers and fishers are an exception to this and they are permitted to use the cash method to file tax returns. If your business has farming and fishing activities, this is important for you to know. Otherwise you might want to forget about it so that you are not jealous!

The cash method is the simplest method of accounting. It is set up to only record transactions when they have been paid. A sale is not recorded as revenue until the cash is received and an expense is not recorded until the cheque is written to pay the bill. This system is quite simple and when you follow this system, your books are more like your bank statements. However, the main drawback is that the business does not actually know what is going on! There is no calculation made of how much money is owed to the business or how much money the business owes to its creditors. Business owners should not be very comfortable with the cash system as they do not have all of the information they need to make financial decisions. For example, an income statement might show that there is a profit being made, even though that is not the case, because some expenses have not been paid, and thus not recorded.

The accrual method of accounting is the most reliable because all the known information is included in the financial statements. The accrual method records revenue when the invoice is issued, not when it is paid, and all expenses are recorded as soon as the business is aware of them, not when they are paid. In this way, the business owners have all of the information they need to make financial decisions. They know who owes them money and they know who they owe money to. All of the reports include all of the expenses and revenues that have been incurred, not just the transactions where cash has changed hands.

If the business files income tax returns and GST/HST returns, it must file both of these returns on the accrual basis. This annoys business owners. They feel they should not pay tax on money they have yet to collect.

Your business can use the cash method to prepare internal financial statements during the year, but the year-end financial statements must be prepared on the accrual basis. As a business owner, make sure that you know which method is being used. If you are looking at cash method statements, you might want to ask if there are significant transactions that have not been included. This question could save you from making a mistake.

Cost Principle: Why Your Financial Statements May Not Show Value

The cost principle is a central principle in accounting. There are changes to the applicability of this principle that are discussed in chapter 7. As I said, this chapter is about the basics. The cost principle states that all assets are to be shown at their historical cost. This principle means that if a business bought land in 1930 for $5,000, it is still on the books and showing on the balance sheet at $5,000.

It is important to note that financial statements that follow the cost principle do not show value, they show cost. Therefore, it is not possible for a person to determine what a corporation is worth by examining the balance sheet. The issue of what a corporation is worth is an entirely subjective question. In my opinion, a corporation can only be worth what someone is prepared to pay to buy it. This is subject to many factors. The financial statements are objective and state each item at their cost, which can be verified.

When you examine financial statements, you should be very clear about which principles are being followed in the preparation of these statements. You need to know whether the business is showing an asset at cost or at its fair market value, and you want to know how "fair value" was determined. Looking at the notes to the financial statement is a key part of understanding what financial statements are trying to say to you.

Lower of Cost or Net Realizable Value

As with many rules, there are exceptions and clarifications. The cost principle is followed only when the value of an asset is more than its original cost. Once the value falls below cost, then the accountant will write the asset down to its net realizable value. For example if your business owns an inventory of floppy disks, the time has come to write off that inventory. The value is less than its cost.

The decision to write down an asset's value on the books is made once it is apparent an asset or an investment has lost its value. This is one area that can be discussed at length with your accountant. How is anyone to know value with absolute certainty? People who can predict the future with any amount of accuracy are fairly rare.

It is for this reason that some organizations have taken advantage of the changes to GAAP to have investments recorded at their fair market values at all times. In this way, if an investment must be written down one year because it has declined in value it is possible to write it back up the next year if the value increases. Fair market value in these cases is determined by the value the investment is trading at on the exchanges such as the Toronto Stock Exchange.

Objectivity Principle: Or, Can You Prove It?

The term "objective" is used to describe transactions that are factual and can be verified by independent experts. This principle means you cannot record anything in the books of the business without some sort of receipt or proof the transaction took place. For example, you cannot record in your books that you **think** you spent about $1000 on meals and entertainment last year. You need to have all the receipts for those meals as well as some indication of why those meals are a business expense.

Financial statements are prepared from summaries of the actual transactions that are made by organizations. Financial statements are not composed of guesses or imaginary transactions, which might be why some people think accounting is boring.

Matching Principle

The matching principle is also sometimes described as "cut off." The principle, if applied properly, allows the financial statements to be more useful, as you are comparing apples with apples. If you are recording revenue, you also record all of the related expenses. For example, if you rent your organization's premises, you would expect to see a rent expense in each month of the year. You would not expect to see two month's rent shown on your income statement in March because you were late in paying February's rent. The goal is to record each expense in the month in which it belongs, regardless of when it is paid. Accountants try hard to match the timing of when expenses are incurred with then they are recorded.

You are using the financial statements of your business to make decisions. If you start to provide a new product or service, you will be very interested to see whether this new product or service is covering its costs. Unless you are an NPO you want to be sure that the new offering is making a profit.

If your income statement does not include all of the expenses you are incurring by offering the new product or service, then you will believe your business is making more money than it actually is. In later months, when all the expenses are actually recorded you might wonder what happened—We were making money, but now we are not?

This situation arises with a budget as well. If some expenses are not recorded, then the business owner could think he or she has money left to spend when, in fact, there is nothing left in the budget.

The principle is to try and match the revenue being recorded with the expenses being incurred so you have financial statements that are accurate and meaningful. We all believe that we will make better decisions if we have better information.

Consistency Principle

> *It is better to be both right and consistent. But if you have to choose—you must choose to be right.*
>
> – *Winston Churchill*

Consistency is a good thing unless you are consistently wrong or consistently losing money! This principle requires you to record items the same way every time. Basically, this is just common sense.

For example, if you use large white envelopes to mail out marketing material—Is the purchase of white envelopes an office expense or an advertising expense? If you record it as advertising one year and as office expense the next year, then your financial statements are not consistent. Readers might assume that you are spending less money on advertising, when in fact nothing has changed. You also have to be sure that the bookkeeper records the expense for white envelopes in the same account as the person in charge of the budget.

Your business sets policies with respect to accounting principles and they should be applied the same way each time. Again, the goal here is to make sure that when you are looking at this year's financial statements they can be compared to last year's financial statements.

There are situations where the CPA Canada Handbook (formerly the CICA Handbook) permits a choice between acceptable alternatives. If you change from one method to another, you have to prepare your statements as if you had always used the new method.

For example, you can calculate depreciation using either a straight-line or a declining balance method. These are two very different methods, and readers need to know which method is being used. See chapter 9 for more information .

If you see a note to the financial statements stating that some figures have been restated to conform to the current year's presentation, you will now know what has happened. A change was made, and in order for the financial statements to be comparable from year to year, the previous year's numbers have been changed.

Disclosure Principle

If your business gives its financial statements to other parties, such as the bank, funders, or other creditors or investors, you are required to include all material and relevant facts concerning the financial position of your business. Much of what a reader of the financial statements wants to know is included in the actual numbers on the financial statements. However, there are some things that have no numbers. These include the disclosure of your accounting policies on depreciation, investments, and inventory.

Commitments are another example of a note required on your financial statements. If you have a lease for your premises, then the amount you will have to pay in each of the next five years will be disclosed in the notes to the financial statements.

Example of a commitment note

> The business is committed to payments under an operating lease for equipment through to 2030. The annual payments are as follows:
>
> 2026 $12,000
>
> 2027 $13,000
>
> 2028 $13,000

Contingent items also need to be included. If your business has guaranteed a debt of another party, then that fact should also be disclosed in the notes to the financial statements.

Example of a contingency note

> Canada Revenue Agency has advised the business that it is disallowing substantial expenses which had been deducted for tax purposes. In the opinion of management these assessments are without merit. It is not possible at this time to make an estimate of the amount of additional taxes which may be owing, accordingly no provision has been made in these financial statements.

There is also a requirement to disclose anything that has happened, since the date of the preparation of the financial statements that would have a significant impact on your business. Subsequent events are only disclosed in the notes to the financial statements when they are a pretty big deal. For example, if your premises burn down after your year-end but before the statements go to the bank, then a note must be in the financial statements disclosing the fire.

Example of a subsequent event note

> *Subsequent to the year-end, legal action was commenced against the business claiming damages of $300,000. The business believes the claim is without merit and therefore no provision for loss has been made in these financial statements.*

Materiality, or Who Cares?

Materiality is the relative importance of an item or an event, and can mean different things to different people. Some people would bend over to pick up a dime; others might pick up nothing less than a loonie. The question is—How likely is it that the knowledge of this event will influence decisions of the users? If the amount is immaterial, an accountant can ignore the effect of all the other principles we have discussed. For example, any items you have purchased but not used up are considered to be inventory. What about business cards? Do you care that you have a partial box of cards at the end of your year that you will be using next year? Will it affect any of your decisions if your office expense is lowered by a few bucks? Do you know anyone who would care?

Materiality is like a "get-out-of-jail-free card." If the item you are talking about is not material, then you can record it any way you like. Measures of materiality vary. Guidelines have been established at 5 percent of net income or 1 percent of assets. However, your accountant most often determines materiality by applying their years of training and superior professional judgment, or so we say.

Materiality is the reason why we do not record a $100 printer as a fixed asset and depreciate that printer for a bunch of years. Most organizations will have set a limit for capitalizing assets and this limit is often an amount around $500. Anything less than that and the item is recorded as an expense rather than an asset. Remember that an asset goes on the balance sheet and increases your assets and your equity and an expense reduces your income and also your taxes, if you are a business.

The purpose of materiality is to balance the amount of time spent recording a transaction compared to the value of the information to be obtained by recording the item properly. Ignoring immaterial items keeps you from wasting time on bookkeeping, unless you really like spending your time on your books! I have yet to meet the person who started a business because they wanted to do more bookkeeping.

Most financial statements are presented to the nearest dollar. Hardly any organizations show statements to the nearest penny any more. In fact, larger organizations will show their financial statements to the nearest million! Imagine a million dollars being a rounding error.

Going Concern Assumption

A "going concern" is a business that is expected to continue operating for the next year at least. The balance sheet of a business is prepared on the assumption it is an ongoing business and it is therefore appropriate to record the assets at their costs, not their values. If professional accountants prepare the financial statements, then there will be a note to the financial statements if these accountants feel the business is not a going concern. Therefore, you may assume the business is expected to continue operating if you do not see a note to the contrary, provided an accountant has prepared the financial statements. See chapter 10 for more details on what accountants have to say.

Example of a going concern note

> *The business will be unable to continue operations beyond the coming fiscal year unless new sources of funding are obtained.*

The concept of going concern is crucial for businesses and NPOs alike. If an NPO loses its funding, then the board has to decide if there is a likelihood of obtaining new funding or if they should consider ceasing operations. The concept of going concern can be applied in a broader sense than just the notes to the financial statements. An organization must always consider whether there is a reason to carry on and whether they have the resources to do so. A business owner faces a bigger challenge if there is a going concern question. It is probable in a small business situation that there may be personal guarantees in place. In this situation, the decision that the business is no longer a going concern means that the business owner may end up paying the bills of the business after it ceases operations.

Economic dependence is a concept that is similar to the going concern issue. Economic dependence arises when one business is … wait for it … economically dependent on another business. This is often the case with franchise owners. If you are running a Tim Hortons you are dependent on Tims providing you with product.

Fund raising organizations are another common situation for an economic dependence note. This type of organization can only continue to operate as long as the funding is received. Thus they are dependent on this funding and this fact should be noted in the financial statements. Any NPO moves from being economically dependent to having a going concern problem when funding is withdrawn.

Stable Dollar Assumption

Financial statements are prepared under the assumption there is no significant inflation or currency fluctuations. This assumption is clearly wrong and is covering up a big lie. The financial statements of a business will include dollars from as many years as the corporation has been in existence. Each year's transactions are recorded in those year's dollars. These dollars are added together on the financial statements as though they were all the same. The retained earnings shown on the financial statements are a combination of many years' transactions. Anyone who thinks about this for more than a few moments will agree that dollars from the 1980s are different than dollars from the 1990s and from the dollars of today. So it is clearly wrong to add them all together as though they were the same. However, what is the alternative? Do you adjust each year's dollars by the consumer price index for that year? This would make the financial statements more difficult to prepare as well as more difficult to understand. Everyone would have a headache trying to figure out what the numbers really meant. So, the alternative is to assume away the problem and treat all the dollars as though they were the same. If only we could assume away all our problems as easily as this.

What you need to understand about this assumption is that the financial statements you are looking at have been prepared using this assumption. If you are comparing the financial statements of a corporation that has only been around for a few years with those of a corporation that has been around for a few decades, you know the assets on the older corporation's balance sheet will be shown at lower numbers, even though they are probably worth more.

This stable dollar assumption does not have as big an effect with organizations that have adopted Accounting Standards for Private Enterprises (ASPE) or International Financial Reporting standards (IFRS), which are explained in chapter 7.

Entity Principle

An entity can be a corporation, a partnership, a society, or a proprietorship. This principle requires that only the transactions of the entity should be recorded in the books of the entity. There should be no intermingling of personal transactions of the owners with the business activities. This principle is near and dear to the heart of the CRA. They prefer each entity record its own revenue and pay its own tax. Typically taxpayers would like to violate this principle by trying to write off personal expenses through their companies.

Business owners with more than one business often need to allocate expenses between more than one entity. For a simple example, I own three corporations and they all operate out of the same premises, so rent should be allocated on some rational basis between the companies. If you were reviewing financial statements and you did not see rent expense nor did you see that the organization owned a building, then you might wonder about the cost of premises. Perhaps the expense is recorded by another company. When you are looking at financial statements for a company that has related parties, be aware that it is possible there are violations of the entity principle and consider the financial statements cautiously.

An NPO runs into this issue when they want to support the activities of another organization. The correct method to offer this support is to offer that organization a grant or a loan. It would also not be correct for accounting purposes for your business to simply pay some expenses for another business and record these expenses as your own. This is something else for a business to think about when the budgets are being prepared.

In order for true comparisons to be made from business to business and from year to year, it is important that only the activities of the actual entity are included in the financial results of the entity.

Conclusion

Generally accepted accounting principles are the rules for how financial statements are prepared. Knowing these major assumptions will help you understand the financial report cards you receive about your business. Being informed about GAAP should also help you understand all the accountants you meet. You should talk to these accountants—they are actually a lot of fun, just a little shy.

Notes and Doodles

Chapter 7. Generally Accepted Accounting Principles Have Multiplied

The Chartered Professional Accountants of Canada publishes a handbook, which is known as the CPA Canada Handbook for obvious reasons. The CPA Canada is responsible for generally accepted accounting principles (GAAP) in Canada. They have accepted this responsibility and are referenced in the Income Tax Act and the federal and provincial corporation acts, and anywhere good financial statements are sold.

You might be looking at financial statements that have not been prepared in accordance with GAAP. Internally prepared financial statements are not prepared in accordance with GAAP. Statements that are prepared on the notice to reader basis are not prepared in accordance with GAAP. In order to get financial statements that are prepared in accordance with GAAP, you need to have an accountant prepare either a review engagement or an audit. The differences between notice to reader, review engagements, and audits are explained in chapter 10.

In 2010, GAAP divided into a number of options, as follows:

- IFRS—International Financial Reporting Standards—for public companies

- ASPE—Accounting Standards for Private Enterprises

- ASNPO—Accounting Standards for Non-Profit Organizations

The CPA Canada Handbook is divided up into five parts now.

- Part 1—IFRS

- Part 2—ASPE

- Part 3—ASNPO

- Part 4—Pension Plans

- Part 5—Old GAAP

This is not good news for the casual user of financial statements as now one must find out what version of GAAP is being used in order to best understand the numbers on the financial statements.

It is however, good news for accountants as we get to spend more time explaining differences and we get paid by the hour!

International Financial Reporting Standards (IFRS)

If the business that you are working with uses IFRS they are probably a public company. This means that they are large and undoubtedly have the resources to help you understand their statements. There is likely to be an audit committee and/or a finance committee and you will be able to rely on them to do the detailed review of the financial statements. What you are responsible for is a general understanding of the financial results.

The big deal with IFRS is that the concept of the cost principle has been thrown out the window. This change means that there are assets recorded on the balance sheet at values other than what the business paid for them. Investments are being shown at their market values—the amounts that you could expect to receive if you sold the investment. It is also possible that fixed assets are being shown at fair values. The business had the choice to restate their fixed assets at value rather than cost when they initially adopted IFRS. They also have the choice to continue to record their fixed assets at fair value, rather than the cost amount, which has been the rule for centuries.

There are other changes within IFRS that are beyond the scope of the book, which could also be interpreted to mean that the discussion would be really boring and technical! These changes involve such things as pension plans, foreign currency translation, asset retirement obligations, and hedging. If the business you are involved with uses any of those things, then you have an obligation to understand how they are being recorded in the financial statements that you are reading.

Einstein was known for saying that if the person talking to you could not explain something in a way that you could understand, the person really did not understand it very well. He explained the theory of relativity as follows—a minute spent talking to a pretty girl goes by very quickly whereas a minute spent with your hand on a hot stove goes by very slowly. That is relativity.

Remember that anything can be explained in a manner that you can understand. Corporations that use IFRS typically have lots of financial resources, which means that you can get all the assistance you need in getting financial answers.

Accumulated Other Comprehensive Income (AOCI)

This term which we defined in Chapter 3, is the account on the balance sheet where you keep the other half of all of the value adjustments you need to make when you start changing the numbers on the financial statements to represent value. Whew! Think about it this way. If your business bought $100 of investments, these investments were recorded at $100 on the books and the other side of that entry would have been to take $100 out of cash. So we added $100 to investments and took $100 out of cash and balance sheet still balanced.

(Aside—you do know that the books of a business must balance, right? So whenever there is a transaction, there are two things that happen so that the books stay in perfect harmony. We call these things debits and credits, but let's not talk of them like that because if we do people's eyes glaze over.)

So back to the investments. You have the $100 of investments on the books. Now what are you going to do if you want to increase the $100 of investments to a higher number say $125.00. This happens because IFRS's policy is to record our investments at fair market value. So you increase the number on the investment account by $25 and the balance sheet does not balance anymore. In order to get the balance sheet to balance, you have to have a place on the balance sheet to put that $25 increase in value. This is the role of the AOCI account, which is where you put the unrealized gains and losses when you arbitrarily change the numbers on the financial statements from cost to value. It is called the unrealized half of the fair value adjustments but I call it the "fake half." So when you make changes to the investment account, you also make a change to the AOCI account so that the balance sheet continues to balance and the world remains in perfect harmony.

The change to using IFRS as a set of accounting principles means that the financial statements show numbers that are closer to being the amount of money a business would receive if they actually sold the assets. Some people feel that the fair value of the assets is more important than their cost. However, what you are giving up by using fair value on our financial statements instead of cost is that you are now recording an increase in value before you have received it. This is called an unrealized gain (or loss). There is no real change in the equity of a business until the asset is sold. Recording value also increases the subjectivity of the numbers. We can all agree on how much something cost, but we would not all agree on how much something is worth.

A business owner should be aware if a business has a policy of recording unrealized increases in value. This AOCI account is the accumulation of the unrealized half of these transactions. So whether you think this is a good idea or not, understand what has actually been recorded. You need to understand which items are recorded at cost and which items are recorded at their fair value.

Accounting Standards for Private Enterprise (ASPE)

This form of GAAP is only used by private enterprises. A private enterprise is one that has no public accountability. This means no shares that are traded on public exchanges, no public debt, and no trust funds. It should be fairly easy to determine whether or not a business is publicly accountable.

ASPE is a simpler version of GAAP than IFRS. There are fewer notes and the notes are shorter. However, the area of the biggest change is in the recording of the financial instruments. A financial instrument sounds like something complicated and it can be—interest rate swaps, freestanding derivatives, hedges, etc. A financial instrument is also something quite simple, such as cash, accounts receivable, investments, loans, and accounts payable.

ASPE also has a rule that all financial instruments must be recorded at fair value. This seems straightforward until you try and apply it. The application of this rule means that if your business buys a vehicle taking advantage of a 0 percent interest-free loan then your financial statements will be more complicated. Let's imagine that you buy a $25,000 vehicle on a 0 percent loan. What has really happened here is that you are purchasing a vehicle at a lower price than the sticker price. The accounting under ASPE will require you to figure out the interest rate you would be paying if you were paying the market rate of interest. Then, use that rate of interest with net present value theory to figure out the actual amount of the loan that will lead to you paying back $25,000 interest included over the lifetime of the loan. Whew. So the loan and the vehicle are on your books at less than $25,000. As you pay off this loan a portion of the payment is considered to be interest and a portion is the principal. So your books are going to show you paying interest on a loan that the lender says is interest-free. Welcome to ASPE.

CRA also cares about these accounting principles, they are not about to let you take a deduction for imaginary interest. They will require you to depreciate the actual amounts paid.

Accounting Standards for Non-Profit Organizations (ASNPO)

This form of GAAP includes the relevant portions of ASPE and IFRS as they apply to non-profit organizations (NPOs). If an NPO is publicly accountable they will make the decision to follow IFRS, if not, they can use the relevant portions of ASPE. In the CPA Canada Handbook, the section for NPOs does not cover everything. You will have to refer to part three if the information you are looking for is not included in part four of the Handbook.

Sometimes, recording financial instruments at fair value can create trouble. This seems like a simple concept, worthy of our support. However, the impact can be that loans are recorded at a different amount than one would expect. For example, suppose a bank gives an NPO an interest-free loan. Since a loan is supposed to be recorded at its fair market value and the NPO is unlikely to be able to get a loan at 0 percent interest, they must record the loan at a lower amount than the amount they received as a loan. This is the rule because the market interest rate for the NPO to get a loan is much higher than 0 percent. As they pay back the loan, the amount they pay back is broken down into principal and interest.

Let's look at a more detailed example. Our NPO, let's call them Daycare, gets a loan from a charity for $20,000—a loan that will be paid back without interest. Daycare has virtually no ability to borrow money, so their interest rate would be at least 6 percent over prime and maybe infinity. This NPO could not get a "normal" loan. The fair value of this loan is whatever amount the NPO could borrow at commercial rates and pay back. You have to record the loan at its fair value so let's assume that the loan is recorded at $15,000. The assumption is that the fair value of the loan is really much lower because the NPO is effectively being given a grant for the difference between the fair value of the loan and the amount they actually receive. The cheque is written for $20,000 of course so that amount goes into the bank account. The difference of $5,000 is recorded as a deferred grant. As the $20,000 is paid back the $15,000 liability will be reduced and the $5,000 deferred grant amount will be reduced and recorded as grant income. There will be confusion.

As you look at the balance sheet and you see a deferred grant in the liabilities you might feel compelled to ask how it is that you owe $5,000 for a grant. Of course you do not owe this money; it is actually just a deferred credit. Feel better now? If you spend the time to figure out the reasons why the items recorded on the balance sheet look sort of weird to you, then you will be able to understand what is going on. A simple decision that all financial instruments should be recorded at fair value has led to there being deferred credits on your balance sheet.

The funders also may not care for this new accounting principle. They lent the NPO an amount and will have expected that amount to be shown on the financial statements, not some other amount.

Conclusion

Since GAAP now has more than one version, a prudent financial statement reader finds out which policies are in effect. Knowing which GAAP is being applied is the first step. Then they should read the policies either in the financial statements or the policy manual. If there is any terminology or other areas that are not clear, then the business owner should find out what it all means. You may be relying on your accountant who is not actually providing you with assurance services. See chapter 10 for more information on accountant assurances.

Are you in charge of approving financial statements? Are you the director for your corporation or serving on a board of an NPO? If so remember you should not vote to approve financial statements if you do not know what they are telling you.

Chapter 8. Revenue Recognition

Revenue recognition are fancy words for the question—When have you made a sale? When can you record an invoice for goods you have provided or services you have rendered? The general rule is that revenue should be recognized at the time the service is rendered or the goods delivered. If you operate a convenience store, you have a sale when you pass the chocolate bar to your customer and he or she pays for it. This is the simplest of situations. You will remember the matching principle from chapter 6, (If you don't, get back there and read it!) that requires you should try and match your revenue with your expenses. If it takes a long time until you record a sale for accounting purposes, there will be a time when you have spent time and money but you don't have anything to show for it by way of revenue on your income statement.

What if you delay in writing up an invoice? I have heard of situations where business owners do not want to record an invoice really close to the end of a quarter because they don't want to send in the Goods and Services Tax (GST) for that invoice before the customer has paid them. So they wait for a couple of days and send the invoice out at the start of the next quarter. Therefore they have three more months to get the money in before they have to pay the GST. If Canada Revenue Agency (CRA) were to be aware invoices could have been sent out but weren't, you can imagine they would be less than pleased! In fact, their rules indicate the GST is due the earlier of invoice date or work completion date to account for just such a situation.

When you look at your monthly results you want to see everything that should have been billed shown as revenue, and everything that should have been an expense shown as an expense. It is only in this way you can actually figure out what is going on with your business. You can always decide later how you want to tell the story to the government or the bank. First of all you need to know what is going on. No point in lying to yourself!

What if you were a builder? When do you record the revenue from the construction of a building that takes several years to complete? Service industries have similar problems. What if you are working on a project and it is not done by the end of this month or maybe the next? What if, in an extreme example, you are not working on anything else? Your whole month would show as no revenue and it would look like you did nothing but be a lazy lump.

What options do you have? There are two possibilities—one method is called completed contract; the other method is called percentage of completion.

Using the completed contract method, you would not record any revenue until the entire job was finished. You would not show any costs as expenses either. During construction, any money spent on the job is recorded as an asset, known as "work in progress." This asset is a type of inventory and is therefore shown on your balance sheet. There is nothing being shown on your income statement.

In the following example, in table 12, using the completed contract method, a project is being undertaken that will take three months to complete. The work is being done equally throughout that time period and will be billed at the end. What you see is a very simple set of financial statements where the equity is equal to the cash balance before this project is undertaken. As you can see, nothing is shown on the income statement until the end of the project. The balance sheet just shows the inventory and payables building up. You are not creating any equity throughout this time period on your financial statements. You know in real life the equity is not just going to magically appear on the day you send the invoice. If you were to look on your income statement, it would indicate you are not making any money. Is that the case? You are working steadily on a project that, if you priced it right, should earn you a profit. On the day you finish this project, you will record the invoice. It will appear you have made that profit all on that day. This method is not a problem for businesses where the projects do not take long. In these cases there is only a short delay between the work done and the revenue recorded. However this is clearly wrong for a business that has large or long projects.

Table 12. Example of financial statements using completed contract method

COMPLETED CONTRACT METHOD

INCOME STATEMENT

	Month 1	Month 2	Month 3
Revenue	$0	$0	$25,000
Cost of goods sold	$0	$0	$15,000
Gross margin	$0	$0	$10,000

BALANCE SHEET

	Month 1	Month 2	Month 3	Month 4
Bank	$0	$0	$0	$10,000
Accounts receivable	0	0	25,000	0
Inventory	5,000	10,000	0	0
	$5,000	$10,000	$25,000	$10,000
Accounts payable	$5,000	$10,000	$15,000	$0
Equity	0	0	10,000	10,000
	$5,000	$10,000	$25,000	$10,000

The other method of recognizing revenue while a project is being carried out is the percentage of completion method. It requires an estimate of the percentage of the job that has been completed to date. This is undoubtedly why it is called percentage of completion! This method is accepted by CRA and is generally considered to be the most accurate method for projects that take longer than one month to complete.

Table 13. Example of financial statements using percentage completion method

PERCENTAGE COMPLETION METHOD

INCOME STATEMENT

	Month 1	Month 2	Month 3	Total
Revenue	$8,333	$8,333	$8,334	$25,000
Cost of goods sold	5,000	5,000	5,000	15,000
Gross margin	$3,333	$3,333	$3,334	$10,000

BALANCE SHEET

	Month 1	Month 2	Month 3	Month 4
Bank	$0	$0	$0	$10,000
Accounts receivable	8,333	16,667	25,000	0
Inventory	0	0	0	0
	$8,333	$16,667	$25,000	$0
Accounts payable	$5,000	$10,000	$15,000	$0
Equity	3,333	6,667	10,000	10,000
	$8,333	$16,667	$25,000	$10,000

With the percentage of completion method (shown in table 13), the income statement looks very similar each month and is closer to showing what actually happened. The drawback with this method is that it may not always be easy to determine the percentage completion of the project. You don't want to spend a lot of time on accounting decisions unless the time leads you to better profitability.

Clearly your cash flow would be better if you actually bill and receive funds as you are working on the project.

Deferred Revenue

What do you do when you have received a customer's or client's money and you have not yet done the work? This money is not revenue until you have done the work to earn it. Until such time as you have earned it, you have to show the amount paid to you as a liability. That is correct—liability—because you have their money and you have the obligation to do the work or refund the money.

For example, if a customer gives you a retainer or a deposit, you must show the deposit separately as deferred revenue until you actually have done the work. Once the work is done, the deposit is subtracted from the invoice you will send them. When this happens, the deferred revenue changes from being a liability to being revenue.

Some deferred revenue situations can get quite complicated. If you sell subscriptions to a magazine, for example, you have your customer's money before you ever send them a magazine. Then you have to keep track of how many of the magazines they have subscribed for, but not yet received. You need a sophisticated database to make this type of system work.

Sales Returns or Bad Debts

It happens occasionally that a customer is not happy with the product or the service they have received. Suppose you have decided to give them back their money. If they are returning a product, the product goes back into inventory providing it is undamaged, and the receivable is reversed. The amount of the sale that has been reversed goes into an account called sales returns and allowance, or sales refunds. Don't just reverse the sale—the amount of revenue you have lost due to sales returns is valuable information for you to have.

In the same way, if someone to whom you sold products or services turns out to be a thief and does not pay you, then that fact should be recorded as a bad debt, not as a reversal of a sale. This is also valuable information and helps you see what bad debts are costing you. If a customer doesn't pay you because they didn't like your product or service, this is a completely different situation from that where the customer is a thief.

Conclusion

Understanding when the accounting rules allow you to recognize the revenue your business earns is an essential skill. It is one area you need to know about in order to effectively run your business.

Chapter 9. Asset or Expense?—A Riveting Question

Whenever a purchase is made by your business, you wonder whether it is an expense or an asset. Perhaps this is not the first question you ask yourself whenever you spend money, but then you are not an accountant.

Why do you care?

An expense will show up on your income statement and is normally a deduction for tax purposes. An asset will be placed on your balance sheet and must be amortized to expense over a period of time. Generally you would like to be able to do both—show higher assets to the bank and lower income to the government. This is why we have generally accepted accounting principles (GAAP), to keep business owners from reporting whatever they want to anyone who asks. This is also why we have accountants—to provide opinions on whether the business has applied the principles of accounting in the correct manner. You can see how it would be very tempting to report your transactions in different ways to different people. And of course we have Canada Revenue Agency (CRA) also on the job to make sure that the taxation rules are followed. Remember that taxation rules are often different from accounting rules, but the financial statements are the basis for the reporting to all taxation authorities.

So keeping all this in mind, let's discuss the areas where you might have trouble understanding the way accountants think about assets and expenses.

Do you know whether what you have paid for is an asset or an expense? We will discuss three areas where confusion may arise.

- Fixed assets

- Inventory

- Prepaid expenses

Fixed Assets

Fixed assets, or capital assets, are items lasting more than one year, such as vehicles, buildings, and machinery. Purchases of fixed or capital assets usually require more thought than the purchase of something that will be an expense. Generally, when a vehicle or piece of machinery is purchased, an analysis of the available alternatives is made and consideration given to the options. This makes sense, as assets will be on your balance sheet for a long time while expenses are gone in a year.

When you purchase an item that lasts longer than a year and costs more than $500, most businesses would consider that to be an asset. This amount should be shown on the balance sheet and not on the income statement.

Your company needs to establish a policy governing the value of a repair and whether it should be considered an expense or an asset. Many small businesses use $500 as the cut off—if a repair is less than that, it is an expense; if it is more, it is an asset. Larger businesses may establish their own values. If the value is applied consistently, then usually Canada Revenue Agency (CRA) will accept it for taxation purposes.

There are some cases where the difference between assets and expenses is not clear. The most common of these variations is in the repairs area. A small repair is generally considered to be an expense, for example, you have a plumber come in to your business to fix a leaking sink. The decision is less clear if the plumber replaces the sink. You have now purchased something that will generally last for longer than a year, so is it an asset? In this situation, if you replace the sink, you are now throwing away a sink you had set up as an asset. This is where materiality is considered.

Let's now consider the case of a roof repair on a building. These repairs tend to be more expensive than other types of repairs and will extend the life of the building. Your business has to decide whether the repair will be shown as an expense or as an asset. The following financial statements, outlined in table 14, illustrate the differences between recording an $8,000 roof repair as either an expense or an asset. The first column in the table shows what the income statement would look like if the transaction were recorded as an expense. The second column shows the situation if the transaction were recorded as an asset. If the repair is treated as an asset, then there will be no repair expense showing on the income statement because assets are recorded on the balance sheet.

Table 14. Example of an income statement comparing a repair recorded as an expense or asset

Bob's Big Business
INCOME STATEMENT

		REPAIR EXPENSE	ASSET
REVENUE			
Fees		$68,000	$68,000
Other revenue		2,000	2,000
		70,000	70,000
EXPENSES			
Wages		20,000	20,000
Repairs	More expense——▶	8,000	0
Rent		5,000	5,000
Depreciation		1,000	1,000
Depreciation on roof		0	160
Office		1,000	1,000
Advertising		1,000	1,000
		36,000	28,160
NET INCOME BEFORE TAX		34,000	41,840
Provision for income tax	Less tax——▶	6,120	7,531
NET INCOME AFTER TAX		27,880	34,309
RETAINED EARNINGS *at beginning of year*		8,000	8,000
Dividends		28,000	28,000
RETAINED EARNINGS *at end of year*		$7,880	$14,309

The depreciation that would be taken on the roof repair, if it is added to the cost of the building, is shown separately on the income statement in table 14. Buildings are normally depreciated at 4 percent a year, except in the year that they are acquired when the rate is 2 percent. Therefore, the amount of depreciation on the roof repair in the first year, if it was added to the cost of the building, would be only $160 ($8,000 × 2%). You can see the incentive for recording a repair as an expense—an $8,000 deduction versus a $160 deduction in the first year.

The company that chooses to record the roof repair as an expense will show less income and pay less tax, at least initially, until they hear whether CRA agrees with their decision.

Table 15. Example of a balance sheet with a comparison of repair recorded as an expense or asset

Bob's Big Business BALANCE SHEET	REPAIR EXPENSE	ASSET
ASSETS		
Cash	$1,000	$1,000
Accounts receivable	2,000	2,000
Inventory	10,000	10,000
	13,000	13,000
Fixed assets	107,000	114,840
	$120,000	$127,840
LIABILITIES		
Accounts payable	5,000	5,000
HST payable	6,120	7,531
	11,120	12,531
Mortgage	100,000	100,000
EQUITY		
Capital stock	1,000	1,000
Retained earnings	7,880	14,309
	8,880	15,309
	$120,000	$127,840

More assets (arrow pointing to 114,840)
More equity (arrow pointing to 15,309)

Table 15 shows the balance sheets with the columns of repair expense versus asset. The difference in the amount of the assets is the $8,000 addition less the $160 depreciation expense discussed above. The difference in the amount of the retained earnings has been shown in table 15.

The company that recorded the roof repairs as an asset obviously now has more assets and more equity than the other company, who recorded it as an expense. You can see how choosing different accounting policies can have a large effect on the financial statements. However, all of this has taken place before the financial statements are reviewed by the accountant who does the year-end financial statements and the tax work. Odds are, the company who has expensed the repairs is going to find out they should be capitalized. In other words, it is likely that both companies are going to show the repair as an asset. The amount is certainly material to the company and the roof repairs will extend the useful life of the building. Therefore, most accountants would want to add the cost of the repair to the building and show it on the balance sheet.

Another point to be made here is about the level of assurance on the financial statements. If the financial statements are being prepared without a review engagement or an audit being done, then GAAP will not be applied. In this case, the financial statement preparer can choose to expense the repairs and there will be no further review. So those financial statements will show less equity in the business.

Keep in mind that nothing that is recorded on the financial statements has any impact on the actual value of the business. The building is worth whatever someone else will pay for it regardless of what the balance sheet shows. I don't think it is possible to overstate this point. No one knows what a business is worth until it is actually sold, so no amount of playing around with the balance sheet will change that fact.

Inventory

If you have purchased something you are hoping to sell, then it is called inventory. It is an asset, not an expense. You do not have an expense until you have actually sold the product. Whether it is an asset or an expense is determined by whether or not you still have the product. If you have it, it is inventory and therefore an asset. If you have sold it, then you have an expense.

Ideally your entire inventory is going to turn into the expense known as "cost of sales," because you hope your entire inventory is going to be sold. Once you no longer have the inventory, it is called cost of sales and you get to deduct the cost of sales from the revenue you just earned on the sale. This is the natural progression of inventory, from an asset to an expense. Products that you have available for sale are inventory and therefore an asset. Products you have sold are no longer available to you and are cost of sales and therefore an expense. Note that cost of sales is also called "cost of goods sold" or just "COGS."

Sometimes a company purchases items they intend to sell and no one actually comes along to buy them. In this case, they have excess or possibly obsolete inventory. Should the inventory continue to be shown as an asset on the balance sheet? If the inventory is obsolete, then the case is clear for it to be written off. Imagine you are a computer store and you still have some dot matrix printers around. Would these items be considered as inventory available for sale? These may be bad examples because it is possible they are collectors' items and might be valuable as antiques! What if you are a convenience store and some of your bread is two months old? I am sure you get the idea. How long do you hold on to inventory before it turns into an expense?

What follows in table 16 is the typical calculation of cost of goods sold. You count your inventory at the beginning of the year and again at the end. During the year you purchase new inventory. What you had at the beginning of the year plus what you bought is what you had available for sale. Once you subtract what you still have, you know what was sold or stolen.

Table 16. Example of a statement showing cost of goods sold

COST OF GOODS SOLD CALCULATION NO WRITE DOWN	
Beginning inventory	$55,000
Purchases	100,000
Available for sale	155,000
Less: Ending inventory	40,000
Cost of goods sold	$115,000

In table 16 the ending inventory has been counted and costed at $40,000. What follows in table 17 is the same calculation if $15,000 of inventory has been determined to be obsolete, damaged, or just no longer saleable. This means the ending inventory will be shown at $25,000.

Table 17. Example of a statement showing cost of goods sold with some inventory written off

COST OF GOODS SOLD CALCULATION WITH A WRITE DOWN	
Beginning inventory	$55,000
Purchases	100,000
Available for sale	155,000
Less: Ending inventory	25,000
Cost of goods sold	$130,000

As you would expect, the cost of goods sold has gone up by $15,000. Because you no longer have this asset, as it is unusable, you now have an expense. Sometimes owners or managers decide to write down their inventory with the plan to reduce their income taxes. CRA does not allow a deduction for any inventory you still have on your premises. In order to get a deduction for tax purposes, the inventory you are writing off must actually be thrown away.

Table 18. Example of a summary income statement

SUMMARY INCOME STATEMENT		
	Table 16 No Write down	Table 17 Write down made
Sales	$200,000	$200,000
Cost of goods sold	115,000	130,000
Gross profit	85,000	70,000
Administrative expenses	40,000	40,000
Net income before tax	45,000	30,000
Income taxes	8,100	5,400
Net income after tax	$36,900	$24,600

The summary income statement in table 18 shows what the entire income statement would look like if the write down was made or not. This write down will affect your gross profit as well as your net income. You have a trade-off—less tax to be paid (assuming you dispose of this inventory) since you now have more expenses, but fewer assets as well as less equity if you write down your inventory.

If you are preparing these financial statements for the bank and for your corporate taxes you have two objectives—keeping the bank happy, without paying a lot of tax. This is why we have accounting rules, so that statements cannot be manipulated that easily.

It is a good idea for you to take a hard look at your inventory and make sure you are recording only the inventory items that truly are assets. You want your financial statements to be as accurate as possible so you are making the correct decisions about how to run your business. There is no point in managing your business by lying to yourself.

Prepaid Expenses

Prepaid expenses are a category of expense that is temporarily an asset. These are amounts you have paid for but for which you have not yet received the benefit. If you have to pay for an event before it happens, it is considered to be an asset until the event actually takes place and then it is an expense. For example, if you pay for a trade show booth, you usually have to make a deposit a few months before the trade show. When you send in your deposit it is not an expense. It is considered to be an asset because it is refundable and also because the event has not yet taken place. In the month the event actually happens, you will move the amount in prepaid expenses to advertising expense. In other words, change the asset to an expense.

Property taxes are another example of this. Most taxing authorities prefer to get their money up front. So you will pay for six months of property taxes on April 30. The six months they are talking about run from April 1 to September 30. Let's say that you pay $6000 of property taxes on April 1. You would record the entire amount as prepaid expenses and it would show up on the balance sheet as an asset. At the end of April you would remove $1000 from prepaid expenses and put this $1000 on the income statement as property tax expense because you have used up one sixth of the property tax. If you were to sell the property, then you would recover the tax expense that you paid for the time period when you do not own the property.

Intellectual Property

There are also some situations where you would like to record an asset because you feel that you created something that should be considered an asset. We spoke in chapter 1 on financial statements about the criteria for assets. Remember that you must be able to show that you have a valuable resource that provides further benefits to the business.

Intellectual property is a category where it is unlikely you will see numbers on the balance sheet. Intellectual property comprises items like policy manuals, internally developed software, websites, domain names, and phone numbers.

Conclusion

This chapter has explained how you will determine whether you have purchased an asset or an expense. The next time that you do buy something, pause a moment and think about how the purchase will be recorded on your books and how it will affect the equity in your business.

Notes and Doodles

Chapter 10. Spreading the Blame—Rely on Professionals

There are three official communications an accountant could put on the front of your financial statements—a notice to reader, a review engagement, or an audit. Any of them will cost you money, but there can be a huge variation in how much.

These communications are generally prepared by the accountants who show up at year-end and issue the official financial statements to the shareholders or other stakeholders. Not every accountant can issue a review engagement or an audit. Generally these communications require an accountant to have a public accounting license.

Notice to Reader

The least expensive and most popular communication (Isn't it funny how often those two go together?) is called the "notice to reader." It means that, no matter what happens, it is not the accountant's fault. This is why it is cheap—it can cost as little as $600. For organizations that are reasonably happy with the accuracy of their organization's numbers and don't want to pay anyone to do unwarranted financial inspection, the notice to reader is a perfect fit. It is accepted by Canada Revenue Agency (CRA) and even by the banks in many cases, although I don't think that the banks should accept a notice to reader for big loans.

What follows is the wording for the notice to reader. It notes that the accountant has compiled, but not analyzed or obtained external confirmation verifying your financial records.

On the basis of information provided by management we have compiled the balance sheet of Someone or Other Limited as at August 31, 2030 and the statements of income and retained earnings for the year then ended. We have not performed an audit or a review engagement in respect of these financial statements and, accordingly we express no assurance thereon. Readers are cautioned that these statements may not be appropriate for their purposes.

The down side to this communication is that the report itself clearly indicates that the results aren't necessarily reliable. You might want a little more certainty and the knowledge that you can trust the accuracy of these financial statements. This type of report is really only suitable for owners of small organizations who have the knowledge and experience to determine the organization's results on their own. It is not appropriate for large organizations, where the finances are likely to be more complicated.

Review Engagement

The "review engagement" is another step up the ladder of assurance and expense. It will cost, on average, two to three times more than a notice to reader but it does provide some assurance the financial statements are in accordance with generally accepted accounting principles (GAAP). Remember from our previous chapters that there is more than one version of GAAP now.

A long time ago accountants used to say financial statements were true and correct. No one says that anymore about anything. The world is no longer that black and white. If your business owes the bank enough money, they will ask for a review engagement rather than a notice to reader communication from your accountant.

A review engagement report says it is based on review, comparison, and inquiry. Questions are asked and the answers are evaluated. How do you know you have recorded all of your receipts? Did you reconcile your bank accounts? Where is your list of receivables? Are all these customers going to pay the amount they owe you? Did you count your inventory? These questions are detailed and require the business to prove their numbers are accurate. However, the questions stop short of asking for proof from other parties. If you want that, you'll have to pay the big bucks for an audit.

Example of a review engagement communication

> We have reviewed the balance sheet of Someone or Other Limited as at August 31, 2030 and the statements of income, retained earnings, and changes in financial position for the year then ended. Our review was made in accordance with generally accepted standards for review engagements and accordingly consisted primarily of inquiry, analytical procedures, and discussion related to information supplied to us by the business.

A review does not constitute an audit and consequently we do not express an audit opinion on these financial statements.

Based on our review, nothing has come to our attention that causes us to believe that these financial statements are not, in all material respects, in accordance with generally accepted accounting principles for owner managed enterprises.

You will see that this communication says it has been reviewed. This is one step up from compiled, used in the notice to the reader. Although it is not an audit, your accountant looked around and did not see anything that they could not fix or could not live with. You should feel more comfortable relying on this communication than a notice to reader, but not as comfortable as you would with an audit.

Audit

The audit is as expensive a report as you can get. This communication is likely to be five to ten times more expensive than a notice to reader. The auditor actually expresses an opinion and that is why it is expensive. The auditor must obtain confirmations from third parties that the transactions have been recorded properly. The review relies on inquiry, but proof is required for an audit. The auditor contacts the organization's bank, funding agencies, or customers. The auditor will also examine other third party evidence such as invoices, deposit books, and cashed cheques. The auditor will also attend inventory counts and verify the count of the items in the inventory.

The auditor does all this work because others are relying upon their opinion. If it turns out the financial statements are not in accordance with GAAP, then the auditor will be liable for the losses of whoever relied on the financial statements. This will involve a situation where lawyers get to make money, so let's attempt to avoid that!

Example of the official wording for an audit report

We have audited the accompanying financial statements of Someone Limited which comprise the balance sheet as at January 31, 2030 and the statements of operations and equity, and cash flow statement for the year then ended, and a summary of significant accounting policies and other explanatory information.

Management's Responsibility for the Financial Statements

Management is responsible for the preparation and fair presentation of these financial statements in accordance with Canadian generally accepted accounting principles and for such internal control as management determines is necessary to enable the preparation of financial statements that are free from material misstatement, whether due to fraud or error.

Auditor's Responsibility

Our responsibility is to express an opinion on these financial statements based on our audit. We conducted our audit in accordance with Canadian generally accepted auditing standards. Those standards require that we comply with ethical requirements and plan and perform the audit to obtain reasonable assurance about whether the financial statements are free from material misstatement.

An audit involves performing procedures to obtain audit evidence about the amounts and disclosures in the financial statements. The procedures selected depend on the auditor's judgment, including the assessment of the risks of material misstatement of the financial statements, whether due to fraud or error. In making those risk assessments, the auditor considers internal control relevant to the entity's preparation and fair presentation of the financial statements in order to design audit procedures that are appropriate in the circumstances, but not for the purpose of expressing an opinion on the effectiveness of the entity's internal control. An audit also includes evaluating the appropriateness of accounting policies used and the reasonableness of accounting estimates made by management, as well as evaluating the overall presentation of the financial statements.

Opinion

In our opinion, these financial statements present fairly, in all material respects, the financial position of Someone Limited as at January 31, 2030 and its

> *financial performance and its cash flows for the year then ended in accordance with Canadian generally accepted accounting principles.*

This opinion falls far short of actually saying that the numbers are correct.

Qualified Opinions for Businesses

A qualified opinion sounds like a good thing. In fact, you probably hope that all of the opinions you get are qualified! However, this is an oxymoron—a qualified opinion actually means that there is something wrong.

Example of a qualification for an audit report

> *Because we were appointed auditors of the company during the current year, we were not able to observe the counting of physical inventories at the beginning of the year nor satisfy ourselves concerning those quantities by alternative means. Since opening inventories enter into the determination of the results of operations and cash flows, we were unable to determine whether adjustments to cost of sales, income taxes, net income for the year, opening retained earnings and cash provided from operations might be necessary.*

Qualified Opinions for Charities

However, a qualified opinion is very common for an NPO because if the charity accepts donations, then your auditors are not likely to be able to prove that all donations that were made were actually recorded in the books of your charity. Auditors are looking for independent verification and this would require them to ask everyone in the world if they gave money to the charity.

The only thing that an auditor can do is make sure that all of the money that was received by the charity has been recorded. If funds have been donated but not deposited in the charity's books due to fraud, then the auditor will not know about it. Imagine the case where one of your door-to-door canvassers takes cash and issues no donation receipts. You and/or the auditor may never hear about these donations.

Example of the standard wording for an audit opinion where donations are taken by the charity

We have audited the statement of financial position of Someone or Other Limited as at August 31, 2030 and the statements of operations, changes in net assets and cash flow for the year then ended. These financial statements are the responsibility of the organization's management. Our responsibility is to express an opinion on these financial statements based on our audit.

Except as explained in the following paragraph, we conducted our audit in accordance with Canadian generally accepted auditing standards. Those standards require that we plan and perform an audit to obtain reasonable assurance whether the financial statements are free of material misstatement.

An audit includes examining, on a test basis, evidence supporting the amounts and disclosures in the financial statements. An audit also includes assessing the accounting principles used and significant estimates made by management, as well as evaluating the overall financial statement presentation.

In common with many charitable organizations, the organization derives revenue from (specify type of contributions affected) the completeness of which is not susceptible of satisfactory audit verification. Accordingly, our verification of these revenues was limited to the amounts recorded in the records of the organization and we were not able to determine whether any adjustments might be necessary to contributions, excess of revenues over expenses, current assets and net assets.

In our opinion, except for the effect of adjustments, if any, which we might have determined to be necessary had we been able to satisfy ourselves concerning the completeness of the contributions referred to in the preceding paragraph, these financial statements present fairly, in all material respects, the financial position of the organization as at August 31, 2030 and the results of its operations and its cash flows for the year then ended in accordance with Canadian generally accepted accounting principles for non-profit organizations.

If your organization has an audit with this opinion it is not a big deal. It is a standard type of communication and should not alarm you. If you are not a charity however, a qualification might be a more serious matter.

Conclusion

As a business owner, you need to understand the amount of assurance being offered by the accountants hired by your business. Since you are looking at the financial statements for your own business, you do not need as much assurance that the numbers are accurate. You know what your numbers should look like.

If you are a board member you are entitled to rely on experts, but your due diligence requirement includes understanding what assurances are being provided by the experts hired by your business. It is unlikely that a notice to reader level will satisfy your due diligence requirement, as you have no reason to rely on this communication. It does not provide an opinion that the financial statements are prepared in accordance with generally accepted accounting principles.

Notes and Doodles

Chapter 11. Financial Analysis

I probably should have come up with a better title for this topic to make it sound more interesting. This chapter talks about techniques that are used to get more valuable information from financial statements. What else can you do besides look at the financial statement?

You could calculate some ratios! Think of the excitement. Ratio analysis is a common technique used to compare one organization to another. A lot of ratios can be calculated using financial statements and some of them are actually quite useful. To get a ratio, however stuck-up it might sound, you divide something by some other thing and in the process get more information. This seems worthy of further exploration.

You might care about ratios if you have borrowed money. Ratios are often included in loan agreements. A loan agreement might require the business to keep its current ratio above one. Let's talk more about this.

The current ratio is the most popular of ratios. All of the bank officials can and do calculate it. The current ratio is the number you get when you divide current assets by current liabilities. You will remember that current assets are those assets that you can turn into cash within one year. The typical current assets are cash, accounts receivable, and inventory. The typical current liabilities are accounts payable and lines of credit.

Current Ratio

Current Ratio = Current Assets / Current Liabilities

(where '/' means divided by)

Your goal is to have more current assets than you have current liabilities at all times. This is important because it indicates you have enough money coming, in the short term, to pay your short-term liabilities.

The current ratio should be at least one to one—a lower number indicates you are unable to meet your obligations as they come due. Any business with a current ratio lower than one is considered to be technically insolvent, meaning it is unable to pay its liabilities as they come due.

Table 19. Example of a bad balance sheet

Bob's Big Business
BALANCE SHEET

	THIS YEAR	LAST YEAR
ASSETS		
CURRENT		
Cash	$—	$9,363
Accounts receivable	55,224	86,551
Prepaid expenses and sundry assets	1,252	1,494
	56,476	97,408
LONG-TERM INVESTMENTS		
Long-term investments, at cost	—	1,640
CAPITAL ASSETS (Note 2)	33,934	40,967
	$90,410	$140,015
LIABILITIES		
CURRENT		
Bank overdraft	$17,657	$—
Accounts payable and accrued liabilities	34,177	26,633
Current portion of long-term debt (Note 3)	16,296	15,134
Taxes payable	7,663	27,840
	75,793	69,607
LONG-TERM DEBT		
Long-term debt (Note 3)	17,250	32,039
	93,043	101,646
SHAREHOLDERS' DEFICIENCY		
CAPITAL STOCK (Note 4)	102	102
(DEFICIT) RETAINED EARNINGS	(2,735)	38,267
	(2,633)	38,369
	$90,410	$140,015

Table 19 (entitled bad balance sheet) shows that the current assets total $56,476, and the total current liabilities are $75,793. This means that the current ratio of $56,476 divided by $75,793 is .74, which is less than 1. This ratio is not acceptable and in fact means that the business is technically insolvent.

Table 20. Example of a good balance sheet

Bob's Big Business
BALANCE SHEET

		THIS YEAR	LAST YEAR
ASSETS			
CURRENT			
Cash		$57,000	$58,000
Accounts receivable		209,811	207,000
Inventory		47,000	51,000
		313,811	316,000
Fixed assets (Note 1)		158,000	162,000
Intangible assets		12,000	12,000
		$483,811	$490,000
LIABILITIES			
CURRENT			
Accounts payable		$89,103	$85,000
Demand loan		52,708	41,000
HST payable		6,000	6,000
Current portion of long-term debt		25,000	24,000
		147,811	132,000
LONG-TERM			
Mortgage		325,000	349,000
		472,811	481,000
EQUITY			
Capital stock		1,000	1,000
Retained earnings		10,000	8,000
		11,000	9,000
		$483,811	$490,000

Table 20 (the good balance sheet) shows $15,000 in current assets and $10,000 in current liabilities. The current ratio is $15,000 divided by $10,000 which equals 1.5. A ratio of 1.5 is acceptable.

The higher the current ratio number is, the more liquid the company. Your creditors are very happy with you if you have a high current ratio.

However, you can be too liquid. If you are holding a lot of your assets in cash, then you could be asked why. You want to have your assets working for you in your business, not sitting in the bank. So a business that holds a lot of cash might benefit from buying more inventory or fixed assets or maybe expanding to new locations.

You might not want to have a lot of excess cash for tax reasons. You have to have 90 percent of the value of your company invested in active assets in order to continue to qualify for the lifetime capital gain exemption on the sale of the shares of your business. My tax book in this series *Ten Tax Traps to Avoid* has a full explanation of this tax strategy.

Quick Ratio

You might notice that the current ratio treats all current assets as though they are equally useful in paying your bills. This is not true in real life. If you are thinking that inventory is not as good as asset as cash then you are correct. A business can write cheques on the bank account, not on the accounts receivable or the inventory. Cash is simply a better asset. Remember that the current assets are shown on the balance sheet in their order of liquidity. Cash or bank is shown first, followed by accounts receivable and then inventory. Accounts receivable are supposed to be turning into cash in thirty days or so, but inventory is two steps away from being cash. First the items in inventory must be sold and then the cash must be collected.

The ratio that is calculated for businesses with inventory is called the quick ratio or acid test ratio. The quick ratio is the same as the current ratio, except that you subtract inventory from the current assets.

Quick Ratio = Current Assets less Inventory / Current Liabilities

If the business has a quick ratio of one or more, then it has good liquidity. Note that the quick ratio and the current ratio would be the same number for a service business as there would be no inventory. There are no cut and dried rules for determining an acceptable ratio for the quick ratio, but clearly the higher the better. This ratio lets readers of the financial statements easily compare the liquidity of the business to other businesses and to the same business over time.

Inventory is a management issue. A business has to have it in order to make sales, but the amount of inventory a business carries affects liquidity and often profitability. We discuss working capital management in detail in chapter 14.

Inventory turnover is a ratio that is near and dear to the hearts of inventory managers everywhere. This ratio is sometimes shortened to inventory turns. In this ratio, higher is better. The ratio is calculated as cost of sales divided by inventory.

Inventory Turnover = Cost of Sales / Average Inventory

Some inventory ratios talk about average inventory, a further calculation. When I speak about averages, I sometimes see some conceptual difficulties. If you want the average inventory for the year for a business, you could do a number of things. You could add together the inventory at the beginning of the year with the inventory at the end of the year and divide by two to get an average. Or you could add together the ending inventory for every month of the year and divide by twelve and get an average. Or you could add the inventory value on Monday morning for every week of the year and divide by fifty-two. Or you could add the opening inventory for every day of the year and divide by 365. Each of those calculations will produce an average. You decide which average is the best average for your business to calculate. If you have the numbers and a computer, then a daily average might be the most accurate. If you only count inventory once a year, then the inventory at the beginning of the year and at the end of the year is all you really have.

Now we have talked about averages—What does the ratio inventory turnover mean? Well as you might have guessed this ratio tells us how many times a year we have turned (or replaced) our inventory. So, if you are selling clothing, you would want to turn the inventory over each month or twelve times a year. If you are selling milk then you would want to have at least a hundred turns a year because you want to be selling only fresh milk. If you calculate these ratios by product over time, you will have some valuable information. If your turns are dropping, then you are either overstocked or you have too many items in stock that your customers do not want. Calculating the ratios lets you analyze your financial information better.

Accounts receivable ratios are also popular. We will talk a lot in the chapter (chapter 14) on working capital about the importance of monitoring your receivables. Clearly, you do not want to sell to customers who do not pay you, but you also do not want to miss out on sales because your credit criteria are too tight. In short, you want to make all the sales that you can to eligible customers.

Days sales outstanding or DSO is a common ratio. To calculate this, take the accounts receivable at the end of a period or any other useful day and divide them by the "days sales." The days sales is determined by taking the annual sales and dividing them by 365 (ignore leap years). So if you say this slowly, days ... sales ... outstanding, you get the idea. If your credit policy is to have all invoices paid by customers within thirty days and your DSO is forty-five, then you are not doing a good job of collecting your receivables. Some businesses remunerate their credit department based on how low they can get the DSO. DSO should be 30 if your customers pay their bills in 30 days.

Day Sales Outstanding = Accounts Receivable / Sales per Day

Debt Ratios

You may have heard the term "debt to equity" thrown around. This ratio is popular in discussions about leverage.

Debt = Total Liabilities / Total Equity

All creditors prefer a lower debt ratio because it indicates a lower chance of them losing the funds they lent to the business. However, borrowing money creates leverage that can be very important in the growth of a business. If a business is unable to borrow money, it will definitely grow more slowly. Borrowing money can help a business expand. A profitable business that expands will make more money. This topic is explored in detail in chapter 13.

As with any ratio, the way to improve it is to change either the top or the bottom of the ratio. So if you could reduce liabilities or increase equity, you improve the debt ratio. The best way to improve the debt ratio is by earning more profits.

Profit Margin

We talk of margins often. Gross margin is the amount of profit earned on the sale of a product. Net margin (or more commonly net income) is the amount of profit earned after all expenses, including income taxes, have been deducted. The net income of a business is also often referred to as the bottom line.

The net income ratio is the net income after tax divided by sales. This is expressed as a percentage and is only a positive number if there is a profit. We have spoken about profitability before and it is appropriate to calculate this ratio over time and look at the trend. If your business still rented video tapes, I suspect that you would have seen your profitability decline over time.

Net Income Ratio = Net Income after Taxes / Sales

Other Techniques

You may want to take the financial statements and analyze them using spreadsheet software. In this way, you can compare items like the percentage increase of each expense year over year, or the percentage each expense is of sales. You can even set up each of the ratios we have discussed in this book and compare them over a number of years or months.

The key is to find the information that you need to know in order to manage your business and get that information from your accounting system.

Comparative Numbers

Financial statements are usually prepared on a comparative basis, comparing the current year to the previous year. When you review the financial statements, what should you question? You should ask about any differences between the two years being compared. For example, if your advertising expense has gone from $5,000 to $15,000 you will probably know why. If there was a corresponding increase in sales, then you will feel much better about why you spent that money.

Conclusion

Financial analysis is a vital part of any organization. The ability to understand the organization's financial situation is obviously critical to managing it. Calculating a few ratios and performing other analysis helps to deepen this important understanding.

Notes and Doodles

Chapter 12. Types of Financing

There is a lot of information in this book about financing. This chapter explains the varieties of financing that are available to organizations. Chapter 13 discusses why you should use financing for your business and the criteria that creditors will use before they decide to lend you money.

In this chapter, we explain the types of financing you may see on a balance sheet. The top of the balance sheet shows assets and the bottom of the balance sheet shows liabilities and equity. Not by coincidence, the comment is often made that the assets are financed either by debt, by equity or by a combination of debt and equity. This is true because the amount of assets is always exactly equal to the total of the liabilities and the equity of the organization.

When assets are being purchased, you need to decide how these assets are going to be paid for. Are you going to borrow money or pay

for the asset with your own money? If you finance, you are choosing to finance with debt or finance with equity. Equity builds up in a business through retained earnings. Retained earnings are much what they sound like—earnings retained within the business. Retained earnings build up when a business spends less money than it makes each year. The decision to leave money in a business is made when the shareholders are comfortable that investing in the business is the best use of their money.

Debt is the type of financing where creditors are paid back the amount they have loaned to your business, plus interest, at the agreed amount over the term of the loan. Creditors do not normally become owners of the business.

Equity financing is provided by investors who buy shares in your company. When they sell the shares, these investors receive the investment back. Equity investors can receive dividends and have the possibility of capital gains if they are able to sell their shares for more than they paid for them.

We are going to start this chapter's discussion with debt.

Types of Debt Financing

There are a number of basic types of debt financing.

- Mortgages
- Bank term loans
- Bank line of credit
- Accounts payable
- Leasing
- Related party borrowing

Mortgages

A mortgage is a loan that is used to finance capital assets. It is provided by banks and institutional lenders, typically for a term of between fifteen and twenty-five years. A mortgage is always secured by an asset of some description, most commonly a house or a building.

Many individuals own a home that is being financed by a mortgage. Payments are made regularly, typically monthly or bimonthly. At some point, the mortgage is paid off and the individual owns the house free and clear. Most people plan to pay off their mortgage and have 100 percent equity in their home.

The acquisition of a building in a business is a classic example of creating equity in an asset. A business buys a building and pays for it over a long period of time. This is a great use of debt because you are paying for something that is increasing in value.

A mortgage is not a difficult loan to get from a bank, primarily because the security is so good. A building is always where you left it. Land and buildings do not generally decrease in value although it has happened in certain markets.

Chapter 13 talks about the criteria that bankers use to determine whether they are going to lend anyone money. When you read that chapter, remember this discussion. Security is a big part of the credit criteria and land and buildings provide excellent security.

A mortgage is the best choice for financing an asset that lasts for a long time and goes up in value.

Term Loans

A term loan is usually used to finance the purchase of a specific asset. (A term loan is different from a mortgage because the word mortgage applies only to land and buildings.) A term loan is normally repaid over the lifetime of the asset, not longer. This is the best plan for financing an asset such as a vehicle. You want to be making payments on this type of debt so that you are matching the cash flow with the reduction in the value of the asset. You are paying for the asset at the same time as you are using it up.

Term loans are also a good idea for those of you who are suspicious of banks. As long as you are making the payment, a bank cannot call a term loan. This is not the case with a line of credit. A line of credit is reviewed and renewed annually, which means that you might not always qualify to keep your line of credit. If your business has a bad year, the bank might decide that you are no longer worthy of credit. A term loan, in contrast, is usually only called if you miss a payment or break a rule in your loan agreement. If your loan is called, the bank typically gives you thirty days to repay the loan or find another lender.

What needs to be decided is the term of the loan—you want to have an asset left when the loan is paid, not a loan left over when the asset is used up. You also want to balance the amount of interest you pay with the cash flow.

There is a trade-off between the loan period and the cash flow impact. In chapter 13 we have a couple of tables about this. But the trade-off is the comparison of the monthly payment with the interest to be paid. The longer it takes you to pay back money the more interest you will pay but the lower the monthly payment will be. So figure out how much you can afford to pay each month and stretch out the term of the loan to suit that payment.

A good option is to have a loan with a fixed payment that you can afford to make each month and a provision in the loan agreement that allows you to make extra payments if you have extra cash flow. That way, you will be able reduce your interest costs over the lifetime of the loan. If you have the cash flow to make extra payments and you are not committing yourself to a monthly payment that might be difficult to maintain.

Line of Credit

A line of credit is used to finance assets such as accounts receivable and inventory. This is the type of loan that will vary in amount throughout the operating year of the enterprise. A line of credit is used to finance the build-up of inventory and accounts receivable during periods just prior to heavy demand. As the inventory is sold and the accounts receivable collected, the line of credit is paid off. There is not usually a fixed repayment amount on a line of credit. Payments are made as funds are available and interest is charged on the average balance during each month.

It is common to be able to finance 50 percent or less of the cost of your inventory and 75 percent or less of receivables that are less than 90 days old. (Therefore, if you have inventory of $20,000 at cost, the bank will usually let you borrow $10,000 on your line of credit.) Inventory and receivables provide the security for the line of credit if the bank agrees that these assets have sufficient value. In smaller organizations or new businesses, the business owner often will be asked to personally guarantee a line of credit.

Lines of credit can also be used to purchase assets such as vehicles or computers. I am not a fan of this practice. What tends to happen is that regular payments are not made on the line of credit and the business still has a line of credit outstanding when the asset is no longer of any use.

There are lines of credit that are not secured by receivables or by inventory. Sometimes a line of credit is secured by a fixed asset and therefore inventory or receivables do not need to be calculated to support the line of credit. This is known as an equity line of credit, which has less administration.

For example, some banks require you to fill in a schedule each month showing your receivables and your inventory at the end of the month. They will then do a calculation, as mentioned, that calculates 75 percent of the receivables that are less than 90 days old and 50 percent of inventory. If your line of credit balance is higher than the sum of those two figures, you will be forced to repay that portion of the line of credit from other funds. This monthly reporting can be a real pain in the butt for organizations to calculate. The ability to eliminate a monthly calculation by putting up a fixed asset as security or by offering a personal guarantee can be very tempting and may also lead to a lower interest rate being charged on the line of credit.

If your line of credit is renewable each year, you do not have the protection of a term loan. Use a line of credit for receivables and inventory financing—not to finance losses. Think of it this way, when your receivables and inventory are high, your line of credit will be as well. When you sell inventory and get paid for receivables, the line of credit will go down as you deposit the cash. A high line of credit will have a large amount of inventory and/or receivables supporting it.

If your line of credit is at its maximum and does not vary in amount during the year then this is what is called permanent financing. You might benefit from "terming it out," which means that you start making payments on the line to reduce its amount. Another possibility is that your line of credit is maxed out because it is not large enough. This is a happier story than the permanent financing issue. If the line is simply not large enough, then you need to sit down with your banker and financial advisor and get the line increased so that it meets your needs. This happens when a business is growing quickly.

Accounts Payable Financing

Accounts payable is the amount that you owe to your suppliers. Accounts payable financing is appropriate for situations where you need to purchase items that are used in your business and you are able to pay for them within thirty days. When you buy inventory, you usually get thirty days to pay. If you sell the inventory in this time period then no problem. If it takes longer to sell the items, then the payments would be made from your line of credit.

Accounts payable financing is what every business has between the time you receive services and the time you make the payment. Most suppliers will give you thirty days without charging interest. This means that as long as you pay the bill by the due date, there are no additional charges. If you do not pay within the allotted time frame, then the company charges you interest, often at high rates.

Example of a typical line on an invoice about payment due

Payment due in 30 days; interest charged at 2% per month after 30 days.

This is, in effect, an interest rate of over 24 percent per year.

Some businesses are able to get longer terms than thirty days from their suppliers. Some businesses just take longer to pay and get away with it because they are larger suppliers. You can get longer terms sometimes simply by asking—you never know until you inquire. As a business improves its financial position, the business will be able to get better terms from its suppliers.

A new business might be required to get products sent to them on a cash on delivery (COD) basis. Once the business has been around for a while, it will be possible to establish credit with a number of suppliers.

Leasing

Leasing companies purchase the asset you want and then charge you a monthly payment, which includes interest. This payment is usually a higher interest rate than a bank. Leasing is a popular choice for businesses who wish to obtain the use of vehicles. You need to consider the lease agreement because it contains a number of special rules.

If you have ever looked at a vehicle lease agreement, you know it is on long paper and the font is small. The rules in the agreement are often overlooked, particularly if you sign the lease agreement without reading it. There is always a rule about how many kilometres the vehicle can be driven during the term of the lease. For a business owner, the number of kilometres allowed is often not enough. So what happens when you drive the vehicle further than you are supposed to? Well, there is a cost. Typically, the lease agreement will specify a number of cents per kilometre. This can really add up and I have had clients who parked their vehicles before the lease was over so they did not incur any more charges.

The lease also often includes an excess wear and tear clause. The owners of the vehicle want you to turn the vehicle back to them in a reasonable condition. If they feel there has been excess wear and tear and the vehicle will need to be cleaned up, then they will charge you an extra fee. This is something else that you agreed to when you signed the lease agreement. There may be no way to appeal the owner's decision that the vehicle has been abused more than is normal. The thing to remember about leasing is that you are driving someone else's vehicle so you have to abide by their rules.

Some leases have a rule, also in the fine print on the back of the lease agreement, that you may not drive the car out of the country. Presumably because the rules of Canada do not apply once you have left the country. It is a great idea to read carefully everything that you sign.

The HST will be higher if you lease than if you bought, because it will be charged on the total payment, which includes interest. If you make a purchase of a car using a term loan, then you will pay HST on the purchase price. If you make a purchase using a lease, the HST is added to the actual lease payment, which of course includes interest. This is not a relevant issue if your business is registered for HST and the vehicle is being driven 100 percent for business and therefore receives all of its HST back. It can be significant for individuals and businesses that have not registered and are therefore not able to have the HST refunded.

Leasing is often chosen because of a lower monthly cost than a purchase. The financial decision is based on the overall cost of owning a vehicle and the cheapest way to finance it. If you have no problem driving a car that is four years old, then if you purchase you could have the opportunity to drive a vehicle after it is completely payment free. This is the best financial place to be, you have use of an asset that you totally own and is not costing you any money. However, there are people who get wrapped up in the perception of a vehicle not its utility, and they are not happy driving a vehicle that is old. They want to always drive a vehicle that is less than three years old because of how that makes them feel. This is not a financial decision; this is maybe a hormonal decision.

When you are dealing with money, not every decision made is a rational one and not everything is about money or taxes. Sometimes people have to drive a car that makes them happy, even if it costs a lot and it not practical. I drive a red sports car that does not really have a back seat. I could own a car that provides basic transportation for a lower cost, but driving that car makes me smile. Every time I see it I think, "What a pretty car!" So I drive it—the decision was not about the miles per gallon or the cost of the insurance. But here is the key point—I am not trying to tell people that my decision to drive a red sports car is a financial decision!

There are tax implications to the vehicle financing decision. Sometimes people tell me that leasing is the best choice for tax purposes. They get this information from the car salesperson. First question I have is why would you be taking tax advice from anyone other than the person who does your tax work! You will get a deduction for the business percentage of whatever you spend on vehicles, so the only way that leasing is "better" is if it costs more. This is not normally how we think about better for taxes.

If you want to save taxes by increasing your expenses, I would be pleased to send you a bill. I see it as a win-win situation.

Type of Asset to be Financed	Type of Financing Recommended
Inventory	Line of credit
Accounts receivable	Line of credit
Equipment	Term loan or leasing
Building or land	Mortgage

This concludes the discussion of the types of debt financing. Debt financing is provided by those whom we call creditors, and it costs us interest to borrow funds from these types of people.

Types of Equity Financing

There are two main types of equity financing for incorporated businesses—common shares and preferred shares.

Common Shares

When a corporation is formed, the investors in the business give the corporation money in exchange for shares in the corporation. The investors become the shareholders—in other words, the people who actually own the corporation. In smaller businesses, it is common for one person to own all of the shares. For example, I own all of the common shares of Peverill and Associates Inc., my accounting firm. If the business you run is incorporated and you own the business, then you are a shareholder.

Shareholder investing is not possible unless the business is incorporated. It is not legal to sell shares in a partnership or a proprietorship. When your business was incorporated, a certain number of shares were authorized by the government department that issued the Certificate of Incorporation. The business does not usually issue all of the shares that were authorized. In small businesses owned by one person, the amount of money invested in the common shares is minimal, typically $100. A common scenario is to have 40,000 shares authorized, but only to issue 1,000 to the original shareholder. In that way, more shares can be issued once the company has been in business for a while to obtain more financing.

The only time a corporation benefits from equity financing is the first time shares are sold. Subsequent sales among the shareholders are only for the benefit of those shareholders. To raise money for the corporation, new shares must be sold. Selling shares reduces the percentage of the company owned by the existing shareholders.

If you are considering obtaining more equity financing for your business, it means you will be giving up some of your ownership. If you sell shares to an investor, they then become an owner of part of your business. Initially it could appear that this type of financing is less expensive than debt financing because you do not have any interest to pay. Recognize however that you have given up ownership in order to get these savings.

There is a financial decision to be made here. How much money would you want someone to invest in your business in order to become a 20 percent shareholder? How much would you want if an investor wanted control of your corporation; if they wanted to have 51 percent? This is a very interesting decision, the earlier in the life of your business that you look for investors, the riskier it is for the investor, and therefore the more ownership you will have to give up.

A corporation may choose to pay its shareholders dividends, but there is no requirement to do so. As long as the corporation has equity, the board of directors can declare and pay dividends to its shareholders. This sounds very official, but if your business has only one shareholder the board of directors is probably just yourself. You can have a meeting and declare a dividend whenever you like. I often have these meetings with myself on the way to the bank machine to withdraw my dividend from the company bank account!

As the owner of an incorporated business, you have the option of taking dividends or taking a wage, or a combination of both. Wages are an expense and dividends are a reduction in the equity of the business. This was discussed in chapter 4 (income statement), table 9 illustrated the difference between where dividends and wages show up on the income statement. There are also big differences in the income taxes that are paid by an individual shareholder on wages or dividends that are not discussed in this book. (See my book *Ten Tax Traps to Avoid*.)

When a business is bought, the buyer can buy either the shares or the assets. If someone buys the shares, they buy them from the individual shareholder and they become the new shareholder. By contrast, if the buyer buys the assets, then they buy them from the corporation.

There is another advantage to selling the shares rather than the assets. The Income Tax Act allows an exemption for the first $800,000 of capital gains on the sale of the shares of a qualified small business corporation. This is an individual lifetime exemption. Because of the exemption, you can accept less money for the sale of the shares of your corporation than for the sale of the assets. For a discussion on this exemption, and to find out the differences between how salaries and dividends are taxed, see my book *Ten Tax Traps to Avoid.*

Preferred Shares

An incorporated business can issue more than one kind of share. Common shares have been discussed; another possibility is preferred shares. These shares are usually non-voting and may have other characteristics with complicated names such as convertible, redeemable, or retractable. Preferred shares get their name from the fact that usually the shareholders are paid dividends before the common shareholders receive any. They will also be repaid before the common shareholders get anything, if it turns out the company fails.

Preferred shareholders do not get to vote at the annual general meeting of shareholders and therefore do not play a role in the selection of the board of directors. This characteristic makes them a good choice for getting money from relatives for a business. The relative gets shares without any guarantee they will get their money back, they don't get to vote, and they may never get dividends. This is a good investment only for people who love you, and in fact is often called love money!

Preferred shares are not just for relatives. Larger corporations may issue a number of different series of preferred shares. A preferred shareholder can be issued shares that have a guaranteed dividend payment. Certain investors prefer shares over interest-bearing investments because of the preferential tax treatment of dividends in Canada.

Public Companies

Once your business grows to the extent that you have fifty or more shareholders, then you are considered to be a public company. The shares of your company could be traded in the stock market.

In the stock market, there are at least two different kinds of shareholders—those who want dividend income and those who want capital gains. Shareholders who are looking for dividend income often buy what is called "widows and orphans" stock. These are the shares of corporations that pay a regular, usually quarterly, dividend. These investors could buy either common or preferred shares, as both can pay dividends. Bank shares are a good example of this sort of shares.

There are corporations that may choose not to pay dividends, which can mean their shares increase in value more quickly because the income being earned is being retained in the corporation. For example, Microsoft, until recently, never paid dividends, choosing instead to reinvest all profits in expansion of the business. This type of corporation can be a better choice for investors who are looking for capital gains. The investor would buy the common shares, as it is only the common shares that increase in value as the company increases in value.

When you read in the financial pages that a company's shares have increased in value, this means the current shareholders own shares that have increased in value. There is no change to the balance sheet of the corporation, as the corporation does not receive any funds when its shares are traded between shareholders.

Shareholders accept the risk they may not get their money back, as they will be the last to be repaid, if at all, should the company fail. Investors who are concerned about not losing their investment usually invest in the stock market consisting entirely of public companies. Investing in small businesses that are just getting started is usually too risky for them.

Equity Investing for Unincorporated Businesses

A business cannot issue shares unless it is incorporated. This would appear to leave an unincorporated business without equity options. However, a sole proprietorship can use equity investing by taking on a partner. This partner could be active in the business or not. If the partner brings financing but no expertise, then the partner would be referred to as a silent partner. This means that the partner takes no part in the daily operation of the business.

Bringing in a partner will mean giving up a percentage of your business. It will be necessary to have agreements in place known, of course, as partnership agreements to govern such things as how to dissolve the partnership, how to make decisions day-to-day, and what to do when one partner wants out of the partnership. It is important to have these agreements in place before any money changes hands.

If your business is already a partnership, then you can raise more financing by admitting more partners or by asking the existing partners to put more money into the business. If the existing partners put more money into the partnership, it shows up on the financial statements as "capital introduced" in the equity section.

Remember the discussion in chapter 2 about the types of business organizations. A partnership has significant drawbacks if there is any liability because of the lack of separation of ownership and responsibility.

Conclusion

The method you use to finance your business is a big decision. This chapter should have helped you to better understand the options available to you.

Chapter 13. Why You Should Borrow Money

A business borrows money for at least two reasons: to take advantage of leverage—using other people's money to make money for your business; and capital purchases—the business does not have the funds to purchase an asset that will be of use for a number of years. If either of these situations applies to your business, then you should look into borrowing money.

The personal example we have used before in this book is the purchase of a home. Many people buy homes using a mortgage. They pay down the mortgage and eventually own the home. In this way, they have paid for an asset over time that they could not have afforded to buy all at once. This is a key point about leverage. A prudent business owner uses debt to increase the equity in a business over time. In the home example, is easier to live in a home and make payments than it is to pay rent and try to save money.

Leverage is a great idea if you invest in a profitable business and a bad idea if all it does is allow you to spend more money on ideas that do not work.

As with many business decisions, it is important to be psychic—to be able to see ahead and decide if the plan is going to work. There is no substitute for psychic ability, although much has been written about market research and business plans. We should never lose sight of the fact that when we begin to predict the future we are still just making stuff up.

Leverage

An example will help to illustrate the concept of leverage. Think of yourself as wanting to be in the pencil business. You see a market, but you have no money to buy product. Let us imagine that you have talked a supplier into giving you the pencils and you will pay the supplier later. In the first table, you see the effects of the transaction where the pencils are purchased. The balance sheet shows inventory and accounts payable.

Table 21. Step one: Purchase of pencils

BALANCE SHEET		INCOME STATEMENT	
		Sales	0
ASSETS		Cost of sales	0
		Net income	$0
Inventory	$100		
LIABILITIES			
Accounts payable	$100		

As you can see, no money has been made simply by purchasing the pencils. The second table shows the transaction where you have found a customer for the hundred pencils being sold, increasing accounts receivable and sales. The fact that you have the opportunity to sell the pencils at $1.20 each is the important feature of this transaction. This is where the profit is being made. (Sales taxes are being ignored for simplicity.) You will note that we are now using two of the financial statements explained in chapter 1.

Table 22. Step two: Sale of pencils

BALANCE SHEET		INCOME STATEMENT	
		Sales	$120
ASSETS		Cost of sales	100
		Net income	$20
Accounts receivable	$120		
LIABILITIES			
Accounts payable	$100		
EQUITY			
Retained earnings	20		
	$120		

The next transaction reflects receiving payment from your customer, thereby increasing the bank account and reducing accounts receivable. This is a key feature because you have the cash from your customer before you have to pay your supplier. This means that you were right about wanting to buy the pencils—there is a good market.

Table 23. Step three: Collect from customer

BALANCE SHEET		INCOME STATEMENT	
		Sales	$120
ASSETS		Cost of sales	100
		Net income	$20
Bank	$120		
LIABILITIES			
Accounts payable	$100		
EQUITY			
Retained earnings	20		
	$120		

The last transaction is the payment of the supplier, which reduces accounts payable and the bank account. This leaves you with $20 in the bank, no inventory, no payables and no receivables. The money in the bank account is equal to your profit and your equity.

Table 24. Step four: Pay supplier

BALANCE SHEET		INCOME STATEMENT	
		Sales	$120
ASSETS		Cost of sales	100
		Net income	$20
Bank	$20		
LIABILITIES			
Accounts payable	$0		
EQUITY			
Retained earnings	20		
	$20		

The previous example illustrates the benefits of borrowing money. In this case the business makes $20 because the supplier gives you terms longer than the terms the customer has to make payment. The company buys the inventory and sells it before it has to pay for the inventory. In this way, the company makes money **that it could never make** if it did not have credit. This is an appropriate strategy for businesses when they are profitable. It is called leverage and enables a business to make more money than it could without financing. If the business is profitable, then adding financing should enable the business to make more sales, thereby increasing the profits.

In the following illustration the pencils are purchased, but nothing else happens. The inventory that has been purchased is apparently not attractive to potential customers, or possibly the price is too high.

At the end of the month the inventory has not been sold and the supplier charges your business their 2 percent monthly interest.

Table 25. Statements after a month with no sales

BALANCE SHEET		INCOME STATEMENT	
		Sales	$0
ASSETS		Cost of sales	2
		Net income	-$2
Bank	$100		
LIABILITIES			
Accounts payable	$102		
EQUITY			
Retained earnings	-2		
	$100		

Table 25 identifies how leverage works to your disadvantage. That is, when you are using borrowed money to do something that is not profitable. The business has now managed to lose $2. When one of my clients is in this situation, I often hear, "How can I lose $2? I never had $2!" Kind of a zen thing.

A business can lose as much money as it can access through credit. Leverage is a good thing when the business idea is valid. It can be a very bad thing if the business idea does not work out. A business owner must decide if their business idea is worthy of borrowing money to pursue. Having a crystal ball available to see into the future would be a big help in making this decision.

The Effect of Interest Rates and Terms

Chapter 12 on types of financing discussed a trade-off between the length of a loan and the amount of interest that would be paid. You probably know that the longer it takes you to pay back a loan the more interest you will pay.

The following table illustrates the effects of four different interest rates on the borrowed sum of $10,000. In each case, simple interest has been calculated. If the terms of the loan called for the interest to be compounded during the year, the interest would be higher in each case.

Table 26. Effect of different interest rates on total interest paid

Amount borrowed	$10,000	$10,000	$10,000	$10,000
Term of loan in months	36	36	36	36
Monthly principal payments	$278	$278	$278	$278
Interest rate	5%	10%	15%	20%
Interest paid year one	$424	$847	$1271	$1694
Interest paid year two	257	514	771	1028
Interest paid year three	90	181	271	361
Total interest paid	$771	$1542	$2312	$3083

If you consider the last line in table 26, you will see at 5 percent interest a loan of $10,000 would cost $771 and at 20 percent the interest would be $3,083. At higher rates of interest, businesses are less likely to borrow money because it costs more to pay it back. Conversely, at lower rates of interest, it is easier to pay back the loan and businesses are more likely to borrow money. Thus, the government lowers rates when they want to encourage spending and raises rates when they want to reduce spending. A business has to be pretty profitable to be able to pay 20 percent interest and still make money. Maybe drug dealers!

Table 26 gives you the data you need when you are evaluating a capital purchase. Often business owners will do a financial projection without evaluating what will happen if interest rates happen to move up or down. A business owner should consider sensitivity analysis— which is a fancy word for figuring out how high interest rates can go before the business is no longer feasible. Obviously a business idea is less attractive when rates are higher because the idea has to generate more income in order to pay back higher interest rates. Not every business idea is able to generate the amount of profit it would take to pay back funds borrowed at 20 percent.

Table 27. Effect of length of the loan on total interest paid

Amount borrowed	$10,000	$10,000	$10,000
Term of loan in months	36	48	60
Monthly principal payments	278	208	167
Interest rate	10%	10%	10%
Interest paid year one	$424	$885	$908
Interest paid year two	514	635	708
Interest paid year three	181	385	508
Interest paid year four	0	135	308
Interest paid year five	0	0	108
Total interest paid	$771	$1542	$2312

Table 27 is illustrating the trade-off between the principal payment and the length of the loan charged. The interest is higher if the term of the loan is longer. It also shows the effect of repaying $10,000 over 36, 48 and 60 months. If the term is longer, the monthly principal payment will be lower. In the example provided, if the loan term is 60 months then the principal payment drops to $167 from $278 (if the loan is a 36-month loan). This can be crucial if the business can only afford to make the lower payments. The trade-off is one of cash flow over overall cost. The interest will be $1000 higher if the loan is over 60 months than if it is paid over 36 months. However, if you only have $167 a month, you are forced to go with the longer term. This is why it is so expensive to be poor. An individual with little cash flow would pay $1,541 ($2,312-$771) more for a car than someone who could pay it off over 36 months.

In your business, you have to determine how much cash flow you have each month to be able to decide how much you can pay on your loans. It is pointless to start out with high payments only to find you do not have the money to make the higher payments and you have to refinance or have your purchase repossessed. A business owner might adopt a strategy of starting with a loan with a longer term and a lower monthly payment, but make sure there is a provision in the loan agreement that principal payments can be made at any time. This way you have the benefit of a low monthly payment and the ability to make extra payments if the cash flow is good, which will reduce your interest costs.

Credit Criteria

At some point, your business will probably borrow money. You might use it to finance the purchase of an expensive asset or to fuel the growth of your business. Hopefully, you won't be borrowing money to finance losses. If you are in the situation where you are losing money and borrowing to pay your bills, then you should seek competent professional advice to determine if it makes sense for you to continue to borrow money, or if it might make more sense to figure out how to cut your losses and move on.

The process of borrowing money usually starts with contacting a bank. The bank official will want to analyze your business and will ask for your most recent financial statements.

It is important to remember the bank is a business. They sell money. They don't have to sell you money if they don't think you are going to be able to easily pay it back. The bank does not want to take your security—they want you to pay them back with interest. They are in the "interest making" business, not the "repossession of your assets" business.

The lender is looking for signs of financial strength

- Liquidity—Do you have the cash flow to pay lenders?

- Equity—Does your business have more than it owes?

- Security—Do you have something creditors can take if you don't pay them?

- Profitability—Does your business make money?

Liquidity

Liquidity is the ability of the business to pay its bills within a reasonable time frame. Obviously your creditors are the people who care deeply about your business's ability to pay them. So how do we measure this? A creditor looks at your balance sheet to see if your business has liquid assets, such as cash and accounts receivable. Cash is a very good asset and the easiest asset to use to pay someone. So a lot of cash is a good thing for creditors to see. Does your business have more cash than accounts payable? Your supplier's debt is shown on your balance sheet as accounts payable.

Liquidity is a similar concept to cash flow, as it is only with good cash flow you create liquidity. Liquidity is often measured with the current ratio—you will remember that ratio from chapter 11 on financial analysis. That chapter also discussed the ratios using inventory and accounts receivable that are also of interest to any creditors.

The current ratio should be maintained at one or higher, which means that your current assets are at least as high as current liabilities. A creditor looks at current ratios and will only lend to businesses where the current ratio is over one. The higher the current ratio, the better the chance is that the creditor will lend you money.

Equity

In reviewing the equity of a business, lenders will look at your financial statements. Equity is shown after liabilities on the bottom of a balance sheet. In order for the lender to be comfortable lending money, there must be some equity showing on the balance sheet.

Equity often takes the form of retained earnings. You will recall that retained earnings represent profits that have been retained in the business. Creditors will want you to have more equity than debt and there is a ratio for that of course. We talked about the debt to equity ratio in chapter 11.

Lenders often have a target for the debt ratio they have set for a company. They require the debt ratio to be below three, for example, which means that the debt ratio cannot exceed three any time that the bank sees the financial statements. Often when a company borrows money, there are conditions set down by the bank. These conditions are known by the fancy name "debt covenants." A bank can specify that the current ratio must remain above one, and the debt ratio must be below three as examples of typical debt covenants. If you do not satisfy the debt covenants, then the bank is within its rights to call your loan. This means that you have to pay it back, usually within thirty days.

The debt to equity ratio cannot always be calculated. If there is no equity in a business, then the debt to equity ratio is actually infinity, as only engineers can divide by a negative number. The ratio at infinity is undoubtedly too high for the creditors' liking. A business that loses enough money in one year to wipe out its retained earnings will be offside on the debt ratio it is required to maintain. Often the only way around this problem is to talk early and frankly with your bank to let them know what is going on. The debt covenants can be temporarily postponed or there may be another way to make the bank happy, such as offering more security.

Security

Any creditor also wants to know that you have something they can take if you don't pay them back on time. This is called security. Some kinds of security are obvious. A mortgage is always secured by the property on which it is registered. If you don't make the payments, the creditor sells the building. A line of credit is usually secured by receivables and inventory.

Every loan made by a bank is supposed to be secured. For smaller businesses, sometimes the shareholders are required to give a personal guarantee as there is insufficient security in the business. This means the shareholder agrees to pay the loan back if the business is unable to do so. As a business grows, it will have security of its own and the shareholders will not have to provide personal guarantees.

One of the advantages of incorporating your business is specifically to protect yourself from creditors. However, this may not always work. The government, and anyone to whom you have given a personal guarantee, is able to collect money from you personally (if you are a director) even though your business is incorporated. Make sure you understand what security you have given to your creditors. It is possible the bank could ask you to sign a form that gives them an unlimited personal guarantee. This means they could seize any of your personal assets, such as your home, should your business fail to pay back any loans.

In a corporation, only the director is personally responsible for liabilities such as source deductions, HST, and corporate tax. Consider methods of protecting shareholders from this type of liability by making sure that not every shareholder is also a director. All of your family can be shareholders, but only one should be a director and this person should not own the family home.

The bank may also ask for a "net worth statement" from you. This statement is like a personal balance sheet. It lists what you personally own and owe. The calculated difference is known as your net worth. The bank asks for a net worth statement so they can determine whether your personal guarantee is actually worth anything.

Profitability

In order for a business to be able to make payments and pay interest, it has to be making a profit. This means that the income statement must show a net income number, not a loss. Banks are not in the gambling business, so it is likely that the bank will want a lot of security if the business cannot show it is profitable. If the business has been around for a while and is not making money, then it may not matter what security is being offered because the bank wants its interest, not the security.

If the business is just getting started, then the financial projections have to show the business is going to be making money, and it is very likely that the owners are going to have to provide some personal security.

Conclusion

A business owner takes some risk in order to make money. If you see an opportunity to offer a profitable product or service, then you should borrow the money, if necessary, to make this product. Understand the role of leverage and creditors in managing your business and you will be much more successful.

Chapter 14. Working Capital Management

You hear a lot about working capital, but what is it? Working capital is the excess of current assets—such as cash and accounts receivable—over current liabilities—such as accounts payable. If your current liabilities are more than your current assets then you have what is known as a working capital deficiency. This generally means you have more people calling you and asking for payments to be made than you have people to call asking them to pay you.

You find out if you have any working capital by looking at the all-important balance sheet for your business. The place to look is the top of the asset section and the top of the liability section of the balance sheet.

Table 28. Example of a good balance sheet

Bob's Big Business BALANCE SHEET	THIS YEAR	LAST YEAR
ASSETS		
Cash	$3,000	$1,000
Accounts receivable	5,000	2,000
Inventory	7,000	10,000
	15,000	13,000
Fixed assets (Note 1)	6,000	7,000
	$21,000	$20,000
LIABILITIES		
Accounts payable	$4,000	$5,000
HST payable	6,000	6,000
	10,000	11,000
EQUITY		
Capital stock	1,000	1,000
Retained earnings	10,000	8,000
	11,000	9,000
	$21,000	$20,000

In table 28, there is working capital of $5,000, which is the difference between the current assets of $15,000 and the current liabilities of $10,000. This is one of the reasons why this balance sheet is known as the good balance sheet.

Table 29. Example of a bad balance sheet

Bob's Big Business BALANCE SHEET		THIS YEAR	LAST YEAR
ASSETS			
CURRENT			
Cash		$—	$9,363
Accounts receivable		55,224	86,551
Prepaid expenses and sundry assets		1,252	1,494
		56,476	97,408
LONG-TERM INVESTMENTS			
Long-term investments, at cost		—	1,640
CAPITAL ASSETS (Note 2)		33,934	40,967
		$90,410	$140,015
LIABILITIES			
CURRENT			
Bank overdraft		$17,657	$—
Accounts payable and accrued liabilities		34,177	26,633
Current portion of long term debt (Note 3)		16,296	15,134
Taxes payable		7,663	27,840
		75,793	69,607
LONG-TERM DEBT			
Long-term debt (Note 3)		17,250	32,039
		93,043	101,646
SHAREHOLDERS' DEFICIENCY			
CAPITAL STOCK (Note 4)		102	102
(DEFICIT) RETAINED EARNINGS		(2, 735)	38,267
		(2,633)	38,369
		$90,410	$140,015

In table 29, known as the bad balance sheet, there is a working capital deficiency because this company has more current liabilities than it has current assets. Current liabilities are $75,793 and current assets are $56,476 which is a working capital liability.

Without working capital, payments cannot be made and your suppliers and employees become annoyed with you. In order to maintain positive working capital, you need to slow down the funds going out of your business and speed up the funds coming in. There are challenges here as every business has the same goal. Your customers are trying not to pay you right away and your suppliers are trying to collect from you as quickly as possible.

What follows are some techniques to help you manage your cash flow—ways to collect your money more quickly and slow down the money leaving your business. Let's start with the money your customers owe you.

How to Manage Accounts Receivables

Accounts receivable show up on the balance sheet in the current assets section. You have accounts receivable when you allow your customers to have your product or service before they pay you for them. If you have forgotten what accounts receivable are, return to Chapter 3.

Do you need to have accounts receivable? You should not have accounts receivable if you have the type of business where it is possible for your customers to pay you as soon as they are billed. A great example of this is a convenience store. You hand over the chocolate bar as you are getting the customers money. In this scenario, why would you agree to wait for your money? Yet some stores do offer credit with the idea that it will increase sales.

Sales will increase if you sell to people who do not have the money right now. This can be a good strategy for increasing your sales, provided the customers do eventually pay you. If you are increasing sales by selling to people who do not, in fact, have any money, then although your sales may be going up, your profitability is not because you are writing off the sales as bad debts. Selling products to people who do not have any money is the same as giving it away.

So assuming that you decide to offer credit you need to establish some guidelines. There are four parts to your credit policy.

- How long do customers have to pay you?

- Are there any discounts for early payment?

- What criteria do the customers have to meet in order to be granted credit?

- What are your procedures for following up if the bill is not paid?

How Long Do Customers Have to Pay?

You can set this policy to be zero minutes! The convenience store has the policy that people have to pay before they get their product.

If you are doing something that takes longer than handing over a chocolate bar, then you should get money paid to you **before** the job is over. Perhaps you should get some money up front before you even start the work. And you should get progress payments as the job goes on. For example—you may want one third up front, one third when you are half done, and the remaining third when you are finished. You should also consider having different policies for new customers or for certain types of sales. New customers might have to pay upfront for your services until they earn your trust.

Are There Discounts for Early Payment?

Some organizations offer a discount of 2 percent off the bill if you pay within 10 days. If someone offers you this discount, you should take it. It is equivalent to 6 percent a month, which is an amazing interest rate. However, do you need to offer your customers that much of a discount in order to get your money? You probably have sources of financing that are cheaper than this one. Loan sharks could be cheaper than 6 percent for a month.

What Do Clients Have to Prove to You in Order to Get Credit from You?

Do they need a credit card? A credit application with a good credit score and references? How much equity or credit references would you require to make it work? Think about what criteria you are going to use to decide if you are going to offer credit.

What Are Your Procedures for Following Up When People Do Not Pay?

At what point do you charge interest? When do you send the client to collection? Is there a time when you send out a big guy to break bones and scare your clients into giving you the money?

Nothing in this book is intended to replace professional advice tailored to your specific situation. You should consult your advisor before making any decisions.

Some Ideas to Help You to Get Your Money in Faster

- Insist on progress payments
- Hold shipments until previous bills are paid
- Pay your commission salespeople only when your company gets paid
- Send invoices and statements out to customers promptly
- Deposit your collections each day
- Insist on certified cheques from bad accounts
- Accept credit cards
- Consider accepting debit cards
- Consider taking a form of mobile processing
- Charge interest after 30 days
- Establish credit limits for each customer
- Use a service like PayPal
- Offer discounts for prompt payment

Insist On Progress Payments

Insist on progress payments if you are involved in a project that will take some time to complete. In fact, before you take on a project in the service business, ask for a retainer. Why should you start working for someone before you are sure they have the funds to pay you? Generally someone who is not willing to pay a retainer will not be willing to pay or to pay promptly. It is better to find this out before you have invested any of your time, which you cannot repossess.

Hold Shipments until Previous Bills Are Paid

Hold shipments until previous bills are paid. If you are selling a product, make sure your shipping department is coordinating with your credit department. If you are having a problem with collecting from a customer, only ship product on a cash on delivery (COD) basis.

Pay Your Commission Salespeople Only When Your Company Gets Paid

Pay your commission salespeople only when your company gets paid by the customer. Otherwise, you are motivating your salespeople to sell with no regard for whether the customer has the funds. Once you make this change, you will turn all of your salespeople into bill collectors as well. Now they will care whether or not the company gets paid and will not waste their time on sales prospects that do not have cash flow.

Send Invoices and Statements out to Customers Promptly

Your accounting and bookkeeping system can also assist you in maintaining your cash flow. The faster you get invoices out the door of your business, the quicker you will get paid. You also want to make sure your customer statements, which should go out at least monthly, are accurate and sent on time. A statement is a list of outstanding invoices and functions as a reminder of the debt and encourages customers to send in their remittances.

Deposit Your Collections Each Day

The sooner the funds received from clients get into the bank, the sooner you can use the money to pay bills or earn interest. If you are paying interest on a line of credit, each deposit reduces the amount of funds on which you are paying interest. So do not delay—deposit that money today!

Insist on Certified Cheques from Bad Accounts

Once a client has bounced a cheque with you, do not accept another cheque. The customer should then be paying with cash, a certified cheque, or by credit/debit card. A bounced cheque is a sign the company is in trouble and you do not want to be one of their creditors when they go out of business.

Accept Credit Cards

Many businesses will pay immediately if you take a credit card. This is the quickest way you will ever get paid by some government departments. A credit card payment is often made by the individual department, whereas cheques have to be issued from the accounting department and this takes much longer.

Consider Accepting Debit Cards/Mobile Payments

If your customers come to your location, consider taking debit cards. This is instant payment directly to your account. If you are a member of a Chamber of Commerce, Board of Trade, or the Canadian Federation of Independent Business, you may be able to get a lower rate than the normal charges of using these services.

If you go to your clients, then take the Square or any other form of mobile processing.

Use a service like PayPal if your business takes orders over the Internet and you don't otherwise take credit cards.

Charge Interest after Thirty Days

Any company that is watching their cash flow will pay the companies who charge them interest first. They will not want to incur additional interest by waiting to pay. If you do not charge interest, then your customers will be in no rush to pay you. Your invoices will be put aside in favour of those who are charging them more. This concept has been completely mastered by the Canada Revenue Agency (CRA) who impose severe penalties and charge non-deductible interest on all of their "invoices." Therefore, they tend to get paid promptly. We should all have such compliant customers.

Establish Credit Limits for Each Customer

This can be done when the application for credit is made. A customer can always apply for a higher credit limit if their circumstances change. Monitor the credit limit on an annual basis to make sure the amount you have authorized is still appropriate. If you have a customer who wishes to place an order that will put them over their credit limit, you can still do so. However, having the credit limit means you have made a choice to extend extra credit—it did not just happen without anyone in your business paying attention!

Offer Discounts for Prompt Payment

If the client pays within 15 days you could give them 2 percent off. This type of incentive was more common in the past. However, you need to examine the cost. A 2 percent discount for 15 days is equivalent to 48 percent interest. You should only offer this incentive if it your cheapest financing alternative.

How to Manage Payables

The accounts payable of any business represents the amounts owing to suppliers. Most of your suppliers will be willing to give you thirty days to pay them. The goal of a business is to pay their suppliers as slowly as possible without damaging the relationship. Here are some ideas to help slow down the money going out of your business.

- Negotiate with suppliers to extend payment terms
- Consider subcontracting
- Take goods on consignment
- Pay items monthly
- Pay bills on a thirty-day cycle

Negotiate with Suppliers to Extend Payment Terms

Some large well-known companies have a policy of never paying before ninety days have elapsed. You may not have that much clout but you can ask for forty-five days at least. You may be able to get better terms if you agree to stock their products exclusively.

Consider Subcontracting

This will improve your cash flow, as you will get terms to pay a supplier rather than having to pay employees. Employees are generally resistant to the idea of waiting thirty days for their pay.

Take Goods on Consignment

In this way, you do not have to pay for the goods in your inventory until a customer pays you. There is a trade-off here because you will sometimes have to pay more for the inventory.

Pay Items Monthly

Pay items like insurance monthly, rather than yearly in advance. This will smooth out your cash flow rather than having to make large payments all at once.

Pay Bills on a Thirty-Day Cycle

Pay bills on a thirty-day cycle, or at least tell your suppliers that you do. This means that you tell people they will be paid with the next cheque run that is in so many days. You do not want to be writing cheques all the time. Your bookkeeping should not be something that takes up a lot of time. Fewer companies are actually writing cheques so you might have to change the "cheque run" to a better term to make this approach believable.

How to Manage Inventory

Inventory can be a real problem for business owners. If you have too much, it ties up your cash flow, requires a lot of storage, and can cost you interest on your line of credit. If you do not have enough, then you lose sales and sometimes customers. It is by trial and error that most businesses determine how much inventory of each item they need to keep.

A business needs to have good records if they are going to make good decisions about their inventory levels. Answers are needed to the following questions. What do we have in stock? What do we have on order? How much of each product have we sold so far this year and to whom? Really sophisticated systems can often give more detailed information. For example, products such as shrimp rings and seafood sauce are sold to the same customer at the same time. Online businesses can do this on the fly. If you buy something from Amazon, they often are able to tell you what other customers who bought that product also purchased. I bet they make more sales with that technique!

If you know what you have in stock then you can figure out whether you have enough inventory or you need to buy more. One method is to determine how long it takes to get new product and attempt to only have that many days' sales on hand. For example, if you are running a convenience store and you get your milk delivery every two days, then you only need to have two days sales of milk. This is simplistic because not every day is the same. Weekends are different than weekdays and for many businesses the weather plays a role. However, you can modify the concept and apply it to your business. In some cases there may be a discount if you order a lot of product at one time. Understand that to be valuable these techniques have to be applied to each type of product, maybe even to every size and colour.

The following factors are considered when you are analyzing the amount of inventory you should have on hand:

- Expected level of sales
- Durability versus perishability
- Style or obsolescence issues
- Ease of replenishing stocks
- Consequences of running short of inventory

Expected Level of Sales

You are predicting an amount of sales for each product that you sell.

From these predictions, you can figure out how much you need to purchase in order to make these sales. Consider how long it takes to get inventory to your location and you can make your plans.

Durability versus Perishability

A product that lasts a long time is way less scary to manage than a perishable product. If you are selling milk, you can only sell it as long as it is fresh. After that no one wants your milk. If you buy more than you can sell, you end up losing money on this product. Figure out how much milk you can afford to throw away.

Style or Obsolescence Issues

Is your product subject to changing styles? If so then clearly you would be more careful about purchasing large quantities. You want to sell all the inventory you can at the best price. Buying product that you end up throwing away or selling at a discount is not the goal.

Ease of Replenishing Stocks

If you can get new product easily and quickly, then you can reduce the amount of inventory you keep on hand.

Consequences of Running Short of Inventory

If you have inventory that is critical to your production process, then you should always have this inventory on hand. Some organizations will maintain a safety stock. This stock is an amount that you will never go below.

How can you figure out how much holding inventory costs you? The factors to keep in mind are:

- What is the interest rate on your line of credit?

- What else could you be doing with the money you have tied up in inventory?

- Storage costs?

- Insurance?

- Security?

Any amount that is tied up in inventory is not in your bank account earning you money. If you are into your line of credit then you are actually paying interest on the amount of money that you have borrowed.

Even businesses that do not sell inventory can have issues with when to order supplies. For example, how many printer cartridges do you keep on hand for each printer? Why would you keep more than one when Staples will deliver most orders for free? The policy should be that as soon as one cartridge goes in the printer, one is ordered. If the printer cartridge is running out and there is no extra one on hand, then you experience the inconvenience of running out of inventory. For each item in inventory, you need to figure out how much to have on hand, how much to order and when to place this order.

If your business has inventory, then you need to give some thought to how you are going to manage it. You want to balance the cost of holding inventory with the risk of running out of inventory.

Remember in chapter 11 about financial analysis, we talked about inventory turnover. If you calculate your turns by product and review this information on a consistent basis, you will improve your inventory management.

How to Manage Extra Cash

Imagine if you had enough cash to pay your bills and there was still money left over in your bank account. This sounds like a great problem to have. Don't leave it in your chequing account unless you earn big interest on that account. Think about the best place for you to invest any spare cash. It might be paying down debt, investing in more inventory, or buying more assets for the business.

If you do have debt, then you should compare the interest rate you get on your investments with the interest rate on your debt. Odds are the interest rate on your debt is higher—pay that off before you make any investments.

Conclusion

If you implement the suggestions in this chapter, you will be able to improve the actual cash flow for your business. Concentrate on speeding up the money coming into your business and slowing down the money going out. As with anything, if you focus on working capital management—you will improve it.

Chapter 15. Pricing for Profits

Pricing is the art of selling your product or service in such a way that you maximize your sales and your profits.

Higher sales are not the right goal unless higher sales will lead to higher profits. It does not make any sense to sell more and more products or services if you are not actually making a profit. It's not what you make; it's what you can keep that is important. Selling is moving your product at a profit—anyone can give it away.

If you understand how much it actually costs you to be in business, you will be able to price your product in such a way to maximize your profits. Have you spent any time figuring out the types of costs you encounter in your business? Sometimes behaviour changes when you pay more attention to it. For example, people often change their spending habits when they start recording everything they spend money on. The idea of writing down a $14 cup of coffee in a little book might cause someone to decide not to buy the coffee.

One strategy for making money is to decide that you are going to sell each product at a profit and sell enough products so you have sufficient profit to cover all of the rest of your costs. Let's look at pencils. If you make 50 cents profit on every pencil and you have $10,000 in other costs then you need to sell 20,000 pencils to breakeven. Most of us have more than one product and life is not quite this simple. This is the general idea though.

If you want to make more money, then you have to either sell more products or sell products at a higher profit (or cut your expenses). If you could make 75 cents on the pencils then you would not have to sell so many of them. If you were selling crack, then the profit is much higher and you don't have to sell so much. There are other issues around selling crack of course, and I am not suggesting that you do so, but this is the concept—a very profitable product will make you more money that a product with low profitability. This is not rocket science and is actually obvious, yet many of us continue to sell products with not much profitability. Why do we do this? Is it possible that we think we can make a small amount of money on each product, but sell enough products that we can show a large overall profit? This is an easier strategy to implement if you are a large operation than if you are a small operation. Think of Walmart—they sell high volume, and because of that they are able to get good prices from their suppliers. They can sell at a lower price and make a profit. Your business probably is smaller than Walmart, so you need a sales strategy that is based on providing good service and not necessarily a low price.

All this talk of costs has probably made you want to know more about your costs. Am I right?

What do we mean when we say the word cost? Well, the word cost itself is not very clear, particularly when it is being used by amateurs! A more precise term is the term expense. An expense is some cost that does not have a continuing benefit. We do have an entire chapter (chapter 9) on the difference between an expense and an asset so if you have not yet read that chapter … this might be a good time to do so.

Generally we think of expenses as items like salaries, advertising, rent, etc. Service businesses don't have to worry about the difference between a product cost and a period cost. A service business does not show a cost of sales on their income statement.

For those business owners who sell a product, there are two distinctions. First of all, the costs are divided up into whether they are product costs (costs that occur because you make or buy a product) and period costs (costs that do not relate to a product, such as rent). Period costs are placed on the income statement and expensed each period. The further distinction between whether a product cost is an asset or an expense relates to whether or not the product has been sold.

If you make pencils, then the cost of making these pencils is an asset called inventory. Once you sell the pencils, then the cost is recorded as cost of sales, an expense. So pencils you have are an asset on the balance sheet; pencils you have sold are an expense on the income statement.

If it helps, think of this in a tax perspective. Inventory is not a deduction. Cost of sales is a deduction. So we don't have a deduction until we sell the inventory. Now what costs are properly included in the cost of products you make?

Inventory: What Costs Belong Here?

Inventory is an interesting concept for some business. A service business does not have any inventory, so if you are in a service business and sell no products you can move on to the next section on fixed and variable costs.

Let's start with businesses who are merchandisers. There are lots of businesses who make money selling other people's products. Large companies such as Walmart and Target are called merchandisers; they buy and sell a product without changing it.

Merchandisers include in inventory the costs of all of the products that they have not sold. Included in the cost of the products would be any freight expense that was incurred to get the product from the supplier's warehouse to the seller's store. Any costs that are a part of the cost of getting that inventory to the store should be included in the cost of that inventory. This is not likely to be what you want to do however, because any costs that you include in inventory show up on the balance sheet and are therefore not a deduction for tax purposes. We have talked about this elsewhere in the book. But remember, assets are on the balance sheet and add to the equity of the business. Expenses show up on the income statement and will be a deduction, therefore reducing the equity of the business and the taxes that the business has to pay. Since few people want to pay income taxes, expenses are more popular than assets. In fact, on occasion I have met people who have spent a bunch of money on inventory at the end of their fiscal year thinking that they are saving income tax. In fact what they are doing is using up their cash flow without reducing their taxes since what they have bought is an asset not an expense.

Any cost you incur to get the item to you in order to sell it is a part of the inventory. This includes items such as freight, brokerage, and non-refundable sales taxes. If your business is not registered for HST or is a type of business that is exempt from HST such as medical businesses, then you will be paying HST on the items that you purchase as inventory and you will not be getting that HST back from CRA (Canada Revenue Agency). So the HST you have paid on the items in your inventory is a part of the cost of your inventory. Once you sell the inventory then the HST paid will be a part of your cost of sales.

Now let's talk about businesses that make their products. They buy raw materials and use labour to create a product that they sell. If you were going to try and figure out how much it cost you to make your product, where would you start? An accountant would start by identifying all of the costs that go into making your product.

So let's say you are making soup. You have a recipe for soup and you know how much of each item you need to make a batch of soup and you know how many gallons of soup that each batch yields. So you could calculate the cost of each item and make a calculation of the overall cost of each bowl of soup.

In technical terms, you are working with a bill of materials and you are costing it out. You have to separate product costs from period costs. So for example, you do know that you have to pay rent. But you know that you pay rent each month no matter how much soup you make. So technically what we are talking about is the difference between a product cost and a period cost. In our example, the cost of the items that go into making the soup are called product costs. Items like water, meat, and vegetables would all be considered to be product costs.

What about labour? The hours that go into stirring the soup and adding ingredients, cutting the vegetables, and packing the soup into containers would be considered to be a product cost, part of the cost of making that soup. The hours that someone puts into selling the soup or sending invoices for the soup that has been sold is not a part of the costs of making the soup. Those labour charges are for selling expenses or administrative expenses, not a part of selling the soup. But, I can hear you saying we have to pay this cost somehow. So we need to make enough money selling soup that we are able to pay our bookkeepers and our salespeople. This is a crucial point. We have to be able to make a profit on each bowl of soup and we have to sell enough that we can pay all of what we call overhead. All those other costs, the rent, insurance, property taxes, advertising, etc., have to be paid.

We will talk about breakeven—this is the calculation of how many products we have to sell in order to cover all of our costs. There is much to look forward to ….

Costs: Difference between Fixed and Variable

Accountants like to divide all costs into categories. Accountants going wild!! A favourite category is the fixed or variable calculation. We do this because we want to spend some time thinking about our breakeven point. This is the point at which we neither make a profit nor do we incur a loss.

The calculation of breakeven is important so that we can analyze whether we have the product or service that will attract enough people so that we are actually making money. In a business, the goal is to make money. If you are operating a non-profit organization, you still have to cover costs so breakeven can be just as important. To begin thinking about breakeven, we first have to understand the difference between a fixed and a variable cost. I bet you already have a pretty good idea of which is which! Remember the discussion above when we talked about product and period costs? Well, a cost can be more than one kind of thing. Who knew that a cost could have such a diverse life? Rent, which was the poster child above for a period cost, is also a fixed cost. You pay the same amount of rent for your office whether you go there all day every day or you only visit once a week.

This is the definition of a fixed cost—a cost that stays the same no matter the activity level. So we need to think about this. How much do I have to make to cover this fixed cost?

A variable cost is … wait for it … a cost that varies with an activity level. I bet you could see that coming. For example, sales commissions are a variable cost. Commission varies with two different things—the commission percentage you pay your sales people and the amount of sales. So sales commissions are a variable cost. We stuck-up types would say that there is more than one cost driver in the sales commission expense. A purely variable cost is one that with no activity at all is zero. So if you did **not** make a sale, the commission expense would be zero.

Mixed Costs

Life is not as simple as just fixed and variable however. Some costs are a little more complicated. A mixed cost has a fixed and a variable component to it. There is some base amount that the cost never goes under no matter what. Even at no activity there is a cost, but the cost increases as the activity level increases. Therefore, the cost has a fixed and a variable component.

A cell phone monthly bill is an example of a mixed cost. There is very likely to be a base charge just for the provision of the service, and then there are a couple of variable charges—one for texting, one for phone minutes, and probably another one for internet usage. You might even see roaming charges. So the base charge is the fixed cost and the additional charges are the variable costs. That makes your cell phone bill a mixed cost. If the phone was sitting in a drawer somewhere for a month and not being used, there would still be a cost.

Gross Margin: How to Calculate

The gross margin—also called gross profit—is the difference between the selling price and the correctly calculated cost of the goods being sold. This number is the profit you make on each item you sell. The calculation does not normally apply to services. A service business will not have a category known as cost of goods sold or cost of sales on their income statement.

Gross margin should be a positive number—otherwise you are giving your products away! There are times when you may want to sell your product at a loss. The specifics on when this may come into play are discussed later in this chapter.

If the company wants to improve on that number, there are two basic possibilities. It can increase the selling price, or reduce the cost of sales.

Increasing a selling price is simpler than decreasing costs—at least from a financial point of view, although your sales people may not agree. Here are several possibilities or options to reduce the cost of sales.

- Reduce the amount of material in each product
- Purchase larger quantities of materials and get lower prices
- Purchase cheaper material
- Reduce wastage of material
- Reduce the time it takes to build the product
- Reduce the amount each worker is paid
- Consider subcontracting the manufacturing of part or all of your product
- Consider offshore labour
- Reduce freight charges per unit by purchasing in larger quantities

All of these suggestions are actually variations on a theme, which is to reduce your costs. Some people might also want to talk about the ethical issues of reducing the amount each worker is paid. Although often valid, we are ignoring these considerations as this is a financial book.

Once you have calculated the gross margin, you have a better idea of what price to charge for your products. The next point to discuss is breakeven.

Breakeven Point

Most businesses would like to know how much they need to sell in order to breakeven—in other words, to cover their costs. As with many aspects of sales and accounting there is a formula for this, of course. Fixed costs divided by contribution margin will give you the breakeven point in units. The breakeven point has nearly mythical properties in accounting. The breakeven point divides the place at which a business is profitable.

The contribution margin is another way of saying gross margin, except that it is calculated per unit, as shown in table 30.

Table 30. Example of a gross margin calculation

GROSS MARGIN CALCULATION		
	TOTAL	**PER UNIT**
SALES (of 10,000 units)	$50,000	$5.00
COST OF SALES		
Beginning inventory	$10,000	
Plus: Materials	12,000	
Plus: Labour	8,000	
Plus: Freight	3,000	
Equals: Available for sale	33,000	
Less: Ending inventory	15,000	
	18,000	1.80
GROSS MARGIN	$32,000	$3.20

Continuing with this example, let's assume the business has $24,000 in fixed costs. The breakeven calculation will be $24,000 divided by the contribution margin per unit of $3.20, which gives you a breakeven point of 7,500 products.

The breakeven point formula will work with service businesses as well. You can calculate the profit in each hour of work completed and then work out how many hours have to be worked in order to breakeven.

In service businesses, it is typical for an employee to be billed out at an hourly "charge out rate." This rate is not the same as the employee's cost. In fact, it should be about 2.5 times the employees actual cost, in a professional services firm. In table 31 the employee is charged out at $75 for each hour he or she works for a client.

Table 31. Example of service business breakeven calculation

BREAKEVEN CALCULATION	
Fixed costs	$25,000
Salary of employee	40,000
EI, CPP benefits	4,000
Total costs	$69,000
Charge out rate of employee per hour	$75
Hours that need to be worked to breakeven	920 hours

In the previous case, as shown in table 31, the business would need 920 hours of work to cover both the cost of the employee and the fixed costs. Any hours charged out and collected above the breakeven point would result in a profit. As long as the business is confident it can sell 920 hours of work for this employee, the business will breakeven.

Selling at Less Than Full Price

Why would you want to sell your products at less than full price? First of all, you may not have a choice. If you have product you cannot sell at full price, then you had better try to sell it at any price. When you hold product in your inventory, it is tying up your cash. You have paid for this inventory and you bought it to sell. You traded your cash for this inventory and you would like to trade it to someone else for a profit. If you used a line of credit to buy the inventory, then you are paying interest as well. Selling the inventory, even for a reduced price will allow you to pay down your line of credit.

When else would you decide to sell at less than full price? Let's return to our earlier example about the company selling a product at $5.00 with costs of $1.80 for each one (see table 30). You would assume that after covering their fixed costs, the company could sell their product for less than the full sticker price of $5.00 and still make money. Once a business has covered its fixed costs it can afford to reduce the selling price of its remaining inventory.

Reducing a selling price in order to sell excess product can backfire. If any of the customers who paid full price for the product find out the product is available at a lower price, they may be reluctant to pay full price the next time they need the product. They may actually insist on the lower price. If you have the opportunity, it can be advantageous to sell your reduced price product at a different location or market. In that way, you don't cannibalize the existing market.

Selling at less than full price may also be necessary when you have obsolete or damaged inventory that is no longer capable of commanding full price. It is better to get some money for this product than none at all.

There are also marketing issues that will lead you to sell at less than full price. Perhaps you will choose a product you can sell at cost as an incentive to get customers in the door. Once your customers are on your premises you hope to sell them items with a higher margin. This is called a loss leader. Convenience stores often do this. They sell their milk at cost, but since you have stopped in, you might pick up chocolate bars or potato chips at full price.

How Do You Determine Your Selling Price?

There are two parameters for determining your selling price. The ceiling is what the market will bear. (Why should you charge less than you can get?) The floor is how much you need to earn in order to live. To establish the floor, you work backwards to what you have to charge for your products or services to have enough money left over! Your price must be between the floor and the ceiling.

Having read through this chapter, you can now calculate what costs are required to make your product or deliver your service. You should also be able to determine your fixed costs. With a little experimentation, you can figure out your breakeven point using different possible scenarios. For example, you have $10,000 a month in costs, so you could sell one product at $10,000 or 10,000 products at $1 each. This is clearly a simplification, but you can see the concept.

Different businesses adopt different pricing strategies. Walmart makes less on each product than a convenience store, but they move a lot of products. Jewelry stores such as Tiffany & Co. make a lot of money on each product, but they do not sell a lot of product. So who are you most like, Walmart or Tiffany? If your business is small, it is unlikely you can compete on price as Walmart does. As a small business, you probably will be competing on quality of service.

Conclusion

In this chapter, we discussed costs, prices, and the breakeven point for a business. These calculations are important for a successful business owner to master and to keep doing (as the business changes).

Chapter 16. Internal Control

What is internal control and why do you need it? Internal control is a system. You need it to avoid getting ripped off or making rookie mistakes. I am sure you have heard about employees stealing from their bosses. These situations take place in big and small businesses.

At one time in the lifetime of your business, you were the only employee—you did everything and knew everything about what was happening in your business. Keeping on top of the business in this scenario is simple. As your business grows, you have to keep giving away tasks you used to do. This simple step causes a bureaucracy to grow. Quite soon you have forms! As you give away some tasks, keep in mind the responsibility for running the business remains with you, and no one cares as much about it as you do.

There are a couple of basic principles of internal control. One of them is segregation of function. This means you design your system so the person in your business who has control over an asset does not also have the ability to control the accounting for that asset. For example, your bookkeeper is in charge of recording what goes in and comes out of the bank account. He or she should not also be responsible for making deposits or signing cheques. Inventory is another example. Your employees who can ship out your product should not be in charge of recording the sales in your books. To be clear, one person should not have the ability to steal an asset from your business and also to cover up the theft in the books. You want to have a system where the work of one employee acts as a check on other employees.

There are two types of internal controls—a preventive control or a detective control. I bet you can see the difference. For example, a preventive control means locking up your cheques, preventing unauthorized people from getting a hold of them. A detective control would be to look at your bank statement to make sure that you understood all of the activity.

Consider the case of a cash drawer used in your business by more than one employee. Let's say you have four employees and everyone has access to the same till. If you find out money is missing, suspicion is cast on all four of your employees. This is not fair. You have a system where your employees cannot prove they are innocent and

and you have no proof of who the guilty party actually is, so no one is happy! (Except the thief!) An example of a preventive control, for the cashbox scenario is having each employee control their own cash box.

You also do not want a system that is too expensive. You could hire two employees for each job, so one could watch over the other! This would provide a pretty good system of control, but it would be expensive and you would have a bunch of bored employees. There is a balance between safeguarding your assets and making money.

Do not assume your employees are actively trying to steal from you. The approach to take is to utilize a system where an employee is not under suspicion, and the system does not allow a problem to occur.

As soon as any business grows beyond one person there is a possibility for communication errors to happen. The following suggestions will help keep your business safe.

Internal Control Checklist for Business Owners

If you are all alone in your business,

You should:

- Sign your own cheques (No kidding.)
- Look at your bank statements
- Pay all government bills on time
- Know how much money you have in the bank

If you employ a bookkeeper,

You should:

- Sign your own cheques
- Look at your bank statements before they go to the bookkeeper
- Ask questions about your financial statements
- Look at the deposits
- Prepare your bills to customers
- Occasionally check over the bookkeeper's work

The bookkeeper should:

- Pay all government bills on time
- Examine all purchase invoices and prepare the cheques for signature
- Reconcile the bank accounts
- Prepare monthly financial statements

If you employ a bookkeeper and a couple of employees,

You should:

- Sign your own cheques
- Look at your bank statements
- Ask questions
- Occasionally check over the bookkeeper's work

The bookkeeper should:

- Pay all government bills on time
- Examine all purchase invoices and prepare the cheques for signature
- Reconcile the bank accounts
- Prepare monthly financial statements

A trusted employee other than the bookkeeper should:

- Know how much money is in the bank
- Look at the deposit
- Examine purchase invoices
- Prepare the customer invoices

Be the Cheque Signer

The simplest and most direct method you can use to avoid having money stolen from you is to sign your own cheques. This means you sign a cheque only after you look at the invoice you are paying. If you do your own bill paying, then you already have this control. Many bill payments are now made online—Are you the only one who can authorize a bill payment? Letting another person pay bills from your bank account is the same as making that person a cheque signer.

Do you check each invoice to make sure the invoices are added correctly, include only goods and services you have received, and have the same prices as you were quoted? If not, you should have someone do it for you, and occasionally check their work.

Look at Your Bank Statements

Have your statements come directly to you, either by having the paper copies mailed to your attention or by being the only one who can download the statements from your bank's website. Take a look at them before you pass them on to any of your staff. Glance at the scanned copies of the cheques. See to whom you wrote cheques and if it really looks like your signature. Look at the bank statements. See if there are any debit or credit memos and what they might be for. If you don't understand what is going on in your own bank account, it is easy for you to be ripped off.

If you get your bank information online, make a habit of checking the activity often (every week or couple of days), so that you have a sense of what is going on in your own business.

Check the Payroll or Contract Hours

Know what hours your employees or contract workers are working. You should approve these hours before the people are paid. If you are the person who does all this, then you have a handle on it. If, however, you have a bookkeeper, then make sure the hours don't go right from the workers to the bookkeeper. The bookkeeper does not know what hours were worked and you don't know what hours were submitted. Don't tempt your employees to try to get paid for hours they did not work.

Pay All Government Agencies on Time

Have a system to be sure your GST/HST, source deductions, corporate income tax payments and Workers' Compensation payments go out on time. Use a calendar, pre-authorized payments, or online banking to make sure you do not miss these payments. Not only are there penalties, but missing deadlines can attract the attention of the Canada Revenue Agency (CRA).

Know How Much Money You Have in the Bank

Be aware of what should be coming in and going out of your bank account. This will keep you from writing cheques that don't clear and alert you to any strange activity in your bank account.

The fact that you know your bank balance will discourage those who might want to steal from you.

Look at the Deposit Every Day

Know how much money was received each day. If possible, open the mail yourself and give the relevant cheques and bills to the bookkeeper. As fewer and fewer actual cheques are sent, this step is eventually going to disappear and be replaced by the review of the bank statements. A bookkeeper will be less likely to deposit a cheque in an account other than your business bank account once he or she knows you have seen it. Make sure that direct payments from your customers end up in your bank account.

Know Who Owes You Money

Your accounting system will generate an accounts receivable listing you can look at either online or on a printout. This information should be kept up-to-date so that you can manage your business properly. The listing shows who owes your business money and how long the invoices have been outstanding.

Look at Your Monthly Financial Statements

Your financial statements tell you a lot about how your business is performing. Now that you know how to read them, it would be a shame not to put this knowledge to good use! Ask your bookkeeper or accountant questions about what the numbers mean. If the numbers do not make sense to you, it may be because there is a communication problem or the bookkeeper may not be aware of a situation. For example, you are looking at your financial statements and see that no expense for bad debts this month has been recorded. You know that ABC Construction went out of business and they owed you money. So you ask. The bookkeeper tells you that he or she did not know ABC Construction went out of business and another mystery is solved.

Knowing how to read the financial statements is a good control. Bookkeepers and accountants are less likely to mess with you if they think you know what you are doing. So spend a little time to understand the statements.

Notes and Doodles

Chapter 17. Financial Decision Making

How do you make decisions that require you to "run the numbers"? This is a very open-ended question. When I teach courses on financial management, what my students invariably tell me is that they don't know how to approach the problem. They are not sure what to write down, what to calculate, etc. Of course once I show them the answer, they think it looks pretty straightforward. So the method I use to teach financial decision making is known as incremental analysis. Does that not sound seriously stuck-up?

Incremental Analysis

Let's imagine that you are trying to decide whether you are going to buy or lease a car. What are the relevant numbers to consider?

The incremental analysis concept calculates both possible options and then compares the results. You figure out what will happen if you buy and you figure out what will happen if you lease. You then only look at the information that is different. Whether you buy or lease, the insurance cost would be the same on that particular vehicle, so the insurance cost is not a relevant cost. The same would be true of the gasoline costs. I think a particular vehicle uses the same amount of gas whether it is leased or purchased.

The relevant costs would be the amount of interest paid on a loan and the amount of interest paid on a lease. The impact of the HST should be considered. In a leasing situation, you pay HST on the total amount of the payment, whereas in a purchase situation you only pay tax on the cost of the vehicle. However, if you get your HST back and you are going to have 100 percent business use of this vehicle, then the HST is not relevant because it will all be refunded. This is the general idea, let's talk more about costs.

Relevant Costs

The only costs we care about are the relevant costs. If the cost is going to be different whether we buy or lease, then that cost is a relevant cost. If the cost is not varying with the decision, then we don't care.

Fixed Costs

Remember fixed costs from our discussion about breakeven. In general, you would not consider a fixed cost to be a part of a decision-making process because it should be a cost that is the same no matter what happens. When we are considering costs from an incremental analysis viewpoint, then we need to think about whether a fixed cost is relevant to the decision.

One error that people sometimes make is to divide fixed costs by something. For example if your rent is $3000 a month, you might divide that into how much rent you pay per day. But this is not a relevant calculation. Your rent is $3000 a month; you don't pay it by the hour or the day. You have to figure out how to cover a $3000 a month rent. So watch out for any calculation where someone has added a fixed cost into a price. If you divide a fixed cost by something, you are probably making a mistake in the calculation because fixed costs are not divisible—they are fixed!

Variable Costs

Does the variable cost change with the decision being made? Go back to the question about the buy or lease. The gas being consumed is a variable cost, but it changes with the cost of a litre of gas and with the number of kilometres being driven. So the gas, although a variable cost, is not a relevant cost to this decision because the cost does not change with the decision.

Sunk Costs

A sunk cost is a problem for people. If you have tickets to tonight's hockey game, you have spent the money. Whether you go to the game or not you have spent the money. So if there is no way to get the money back it is a sunk cost and is no longer relevant to whether you should go or not. You have spent the money—the decision to be made now is whether you should spend the time.

Three Columns

The incremental analysis format has three columns. In your buy or lease decision, there would be one column that says buy, one column that says lease, and the third column is the difference between the buying and the leasing. The best thing about the three-column approach is that once you get good at figuring out the relevant costs, you can skip the first two columns and just analyze the decision. Until you develop those skills the first two columns can be very helpful.

Here, we show a simple example of this situation. The sawmill is losing money because it is closed. If the sawmill is rented out, then they will have some incremental revenue and some incremental costs. The question to be answered is how much incremental profit will you make if you rent out the sawmill.

Example of Incremental Analysis Approach

Nova Scotia Lumber (a sawmill) is closed due to a strike. The fixed costs of operation are $15,000 per week, which includes interest, amortization, and management salaries.

A film company has offered to rent the sawmill for one week for $10,000. If the mill is rented, the cleanup costs will be $2,000. Here is the income statement if we rent the sawmill.

Revenue	$10,000
Expenses	
Weekly fixed costs	15,000
Cleanup costs	2,000
	17,000
Operating loss	-$7,000

We have analyzed this decision using the three columns below.

If all you were told was that you had a proposal to rent the sawmill for a week and if you did so you would lose $7,000, you would be likely to say no. However, the correct question to ask is—How much will you lose if you do **not** rent the sawmill this week?

	Rejected Offer	Accepted Offer	Incremental Analysis
Revenue	$0	$10,000	$10,000
Expenses			
Weekly fixed costs	15,000	15,000	
Cleanup costs		2,000	2,000
	15,000	17,000	2,000
Operating loss	-$15,000	-$7,000	$8,000

Using the three-column approach, you can now analyze the decision into a column for the results if we reject the offer and the results if we accept the offer. This will leave us with a comparison of the two possibilities. After you have practiced this technique, for a while you will be able to skip the first two columns and just prepare the incremental analysis.

The problem with the first income statement prepared is that it includes a fixed cost that which is not relevant to the decision. This cost is going to occur whether you rent the sawmill or not, so it does not matter when making this decision.

Make or Buy?

How do you decide whether your business should make something or just go out and buy it? Well, the incremental analysis approach will work for this decision as well. What costs will you be able to get rid of if you no longer make a part yourself? You compare those numbers with the actual cost of buying the part.

We can do this with services as well, which probably has more applicability since there is so little Canadian manufacturing! So how do you decide to give up doing something yourself and just buy it? How about housecleaning? If you were to spend the four hours a week you currently spend housecleaning on activities that you could charge your clients for, then would you make more money? How much do you charge an hour? Compare that to how much the cleaning service charges an hour. This is how you decide if you would be further ahead. Don't forget to add in the costs that you no longer incur—such as for cleaning products that you don't buy because you are not doing the cleaning. There are also additional costs such as keys for the cleaning staff. This analysis works if you are able to sell your time. If you don't have any clients, then you might as well clean the house! You would be saving the cleaning cost.

Dropping Unprofitable Products

Another financial decision to be made is whether you should stop offering a product if you are not making any money on that product. First find out how this loss was calculated. Please don't accept anyone's calculation of anything without asking how the calculation was done.

For example, what if someone asks you if you want to do something and if you do that something your company will lose $5,000. Well most of us would say no we don't want to do that because if we do it we will lose money. There is another question to be asked at this point. How much money will be lost if you **don't** do it? Ask how the calculation was done before you go ahead with anything.

Have you ever heard anyone say—It costs us $100 to write a letter? Who makes this stuff up? How do they calculate these things? What if the person wrote the letter while watching TV at home? What if the employee does not do anything else all day but draft a letter and worry about the wording? There are a lot of variables in the calculation.

If you don't get anything else out of this chapter—remember this— if someone tells you that it costs $$ to do something, the next words out of your mouth should be, "How did you calculate that?" There are a lot of ways to do this type of calculation and you need to understand how it was done before you make a decision.

Conclusion

Financial decision making is all about determining the information you need and the information that does not matter. Understanding any financial report will help you make the best decisions for your organization.

Notes and Doodles

Chapter 18. Operational Budgets

A well-run business will have an annual budget. The budget preparation and review should be detailed if the budget is going to have any validity. Let's talk a bit about terminology here. There are a number of words that are used to describe what sounds like the same things. These words are budget, forecast, and projection. Technically a budget is the name you give a document that you are using to measure performance. So a budget is given to employees and they are expected to achieve this budget.

A forecast is the document that shows what you believe will be the most likely outcome. So for example, a board could set a fundraising budget of $100,000 but fully expect that only $85,000 will be obtained. In a business scenario, often the owner will tell the sales department that the sales goal is $1,000,000 but use $800,000 in their forecast because they believe the $800,000 is the most likely outcome. They are using the budget as a means of motivating the employees, presumably.

A projection is a set of financial statements prepared using a number of assumptions, any set of assumptions, not necessarily the most probable ones. You might also hear the term pro-forma, which is the same as a projection. So now that we have that out of the way—we can talk about more practical matters.

How Do You Prepare a Budget?

There are a number of assumptions that need to be made in order to prepare a budget. These assumptions include the level of sales that will be made; the significant expenses that will be incurred; cash flow assumptions about how fast customers are going to pay; and how quickly the business will be able to pay their bills.

The business owner should insist that the budget follow the same chart of accounts as the financial statements. The budget categories will therefore follow the financial records. When a transaction is recorded in the accounting system of the business it should also be in the budget comparisons. The next question is—How do you divide up the yearly expenses? Do you budget for when you are going to pay for the item or when you are going to incur the expense? If you pay for your insurance expense at the beginning of the year, then do you show all of that expense in January on the budget? Will your accounting system show the insurance expense as one-twelfth of the annual expense each month?

For example, if you have paid for airplane tickets or a conference before the month that the conference takes place, the amount that you have paid is considered to be a prepaid expense until that month arrives and you actually go to the conference. So the amount of the payment is an asset until you "use it up" and it becomes an expense. The accounting records are going to show this expense as a prepaid expense on the balance sheet. This means the income statement does not show this conference expense. How does the business make sure that they take all prepayments into account when making spending decisions? Do you budget the item when you are going to go to the conference or when you are going to pay for it? How do you keep track of the fact that you have spent the money when there is no expense showing in the income statement?

A business may also run into an issue if they want to support the activities of another business. Many entrepreneurs will start new businesses after their first one gets to a certain size! The correct method to offer this support is to offer that business a loan. It would not be correct for accounting purposes for your business to simply pay some expenses for this other business and record these expenses as their own (Remember the entity concept). This is something else for a business to think about when the budgets are being prepared. This sort of accounting can be trouble for a budgeting system.

If you are looking for more information on how to actually prepare a budget, forecast, or projection, I have written an entire book devoted to this topic—*Budgeting Essentials*.

How Do You Review a Budget?

The budget should look a lot like an income statement or statement of operations. The categories on the budget should be the same as the categories on the financial statements that you are given each month. For example, if your revenue comes from speaking and consulting, then these categories will be shown on the budget. It would not be appropriate for the budget to just say revenue. If your revenue comes from sales to commercial and residential customers, then you want that distinction made on the financial statements and on the budget. You need to be able to compare the budget with the past results of the business and this can only be done if the categories are the same.

To review a budget that you did not prepare you have to ask questions about the budget. The first thing you want to know is how the budget for the coming year differs from the actual results of the previous year. What conditions are expected to remain the same and what conditions are expected to change? Look at the line for salaries. Is there an assumption of wage increases? Ask questions about any expense item that is going to be significantly different from the previous year. Are there any conditions you are aware of that do not seem to be incorporated into the budget?

Is there a list of assumptions? If so read them over and ask yourself if you think they are reasonable based on your knowledge of the business and the community.

Only after reviewing the budget, comparing it with the previous year's actual results, and understanding the assumptions that are being made, should the budget be approved.

How Often Should a Budget Be Reviewed?

If the budget is a meaningful part of your organization's financial management process, then it will probably be appropriate for the budget to be examined monthly. The budget should be compared to the actual amount of spending that has taken place to date in the year and a forecast should be made of where you anticipate that the budget will end up at the end of the year.

This process is called compare and forecast. If the business is not interested in looking at the budget each month, then the budget is not really being used effectively. Some organizations only look at the budget once a year, which means they are not using it as a tool to monitor and control the spending of the business.

Budget Revisions

Each business will also have a policy about whether there are circumstances that will result in the budget being changed. Some organizations hold the budget as sacred and there are no conditions under which an adjustment will be made. Others might feel that once it is apparent that the budget will not be achieved because of some unforeseen circumstance, then it is better to revise the budget.

If the budget is being used to control spending, then any change that is made to the budget would only be to replace spending on a certain item or project with spending on a different item or project. Money can't be spent if it is not in the budget.

In the case where circumstances have changed such that the budget is no longer really an effective tool, then the business will decide whether it is now appropriate to change the budget. In a business scenario, if it becomes apparent that a large contract that was forecast to be obtained by the business is definitely not going to be awarded to the corporation, then the revenue and expense budget should be cut. There is no point in continuing to expect your sales staff to reach sales goals that now appear to be out of reach.

Opinions on this do differ, but an effective budget is one that those employees whose activities are budgeted consider to be fair. If an employee has had a hand in setting the budget, then they are more likely to be motivated.

Budget to Forecast

If the budget is being reviewed each month and compared to actual results then an organization could make use of both a budget and a forecast. To make a forecast, take the template that was used to develop the budget and insert the actual results. See what the model says about the rest of the year. As the budget amounts are replaced with actual results you will see how accurate your assumptions were. You are also slowing turning your budget into a forecast.

Conclusion

Putting some time into budgeting will vastly improve the management of the organization.

Chapter 19. Capital Budgeting

What is the difference between capital budgeting and regular budgeting? Capital budgeting refers to the purchase of fixed assets such as equipment, vehicles, land, and buildings. This is the type of purchase that shows up on a balance sheet not on the income statements. Capital budgeting is a little more complicated because it ends up affecting the income statement only through depreciation. Remember the discussion about assets—they are things you pay for that last for longer than a year and generally cost more than $500. Because these items last longer than a year, we attempt to spread the cost over a number of time periods. We do this through depreciation, which has already been discussed in this book.

The regular kind of budgeting is actually called operational budgeting by stuck-up accountants everywhere. Most business owners do operational budgeting because it is the type of budgeting that helps you determine whether you need to increase sales or reduce expenditures.

Capital budgeting on the other hand is about deciding which capital items the business should purchase. This is an area where we often just do some math in our heads and then decide. Or it is an area where we do not make a financial decision. The decision about buying a car often has nothing to do with the financial aspects. We buy a car that we think is an expression of our personality or that will affect other people's perception of us. Even though an older car may in fact work just as well as a new car, we are under the impression that if we buy a new car, people will think that we are doing better and they will be more likely to think we are successful and therefore should give us their business.

We are going to talk about a couple of different methods used to make decisions. When you are buying a new car—How do you decide which one it should be? Or when buying a new smartphone—What criteria do you use to decide if you are going to buy a Blackberry, an iPhone or a Samsung?

First, you should always have a list going of stuff that you will need. How long until the photocopier has to be replaced? The computers in the office are how old? Do you need other equipment in your business? If you are a store, how long until you want to replace racks, flooring, and paint?

The type of capital budgeting decisions that are being made will help determine who makes the decision. If you are simply replacing an asset with a similar asset, then this decision could be made at the lowest level of the organization. A broken table must be replaced with a similar table. If the capital budgeting decision is to replace the asset with something that costs less, such as whether the table should be replaced at all, then that is the type of decision that might be made at a higher level in the organization.

As with many decision frameworks, the more important a decision is, the higher up in an organization the decision should be made. So if the decision is about buying equipment to launch a new product, then the board of directors should be making this decision. Any decision that needs to be made by a board is going to need a bunch of analysis. The board is going to be asking questions about the origin of some of the assumptions.

Techniques for Analyzing Potential Capital Expenditures

- Payback
- Return on investment
- Net present value

Payback

Payback is the most common technique, and one that you can do in your head. For example, if you are deciding whether to buy an annual pass to a golf course, you are going to take the amount of the pass and divide it by the daily cost for a round of golf. You will then decide if you are likely to play golf more times than that. Okay, let's use some easy numbers. If the annual pass is $1000 and it costs $100 to play eighteen holes, then you need to golf ten times to get your money back. If you golfed eleven times, you were better off buying the pass. If you golfed four times (and bought the pass), you ended up paying $250 for each round. Although the annual pass is not a capital item, you get the idea about how to use the technique.

When you are deciding about buying a toaster for your restaurant, you can do the same thing. You decide how long it will take you to get your money back. So if you make $1 profit on every slice of bread that you toast, then a $500 toaster will have a payback number of 500 slices of bread. If a $400 toaster is slower and uses more electricity, you might only make 98 cents on every slice of bread but that toaster has a payback of 408 and is a better deal.

One of the problems with the payback method is that it does not pay any attention to the cash flow impact of the time beyond the payback. Wow, that was a lot of words. What I mean is that the payback technique does not care that the $400 toaster is going to last for five months and the $500 toaster is going to last for twelve months! This is a simple technique, most often used and it is not really very accurate.

The actual payback calculation is to take the cost of the original investment and divide it by the annual cash flow that will be earned with the purchase of the asset. Therefore, you need to estimate cash flow. You have probably determined that when you use these techniques you are estimating the numbers you use to make the decisions. Anytime that you are making a decision about something that will happen in the future, you need to make up the numbers. Even if you use the most sophisticated of techniques to analyze what you are going to do, you are still imagining the numbers, so any decision is affected by that simple fact.

Return on Investment (ROI)

You hear this term a lot; mostly used by amateurs. People wonder what the ROI is on this conversation, for example. Or what is the ROI on having children? If you want the ROI on having children then check out my book *Every Canadian's Guide to Financial Prosperity.*

Table 32. Example of a return on investment chart

RETURN ON INVESTMENT (ROI)		
Net income	$300	60%
Average investment	$500	
Net income	275	69%
Average investment	$400	

Here, you figure out the net income effect of doing something and divide it by the cost. So, back to the toaster. If we have a net income for the year of $300 on the $500 toaster, then the ROI is 60 percent, which is pretty good. ($300 divided by $500)

If the $400 toaster has a net income of $275, then its ROI is 69 percent ($275 divided by $400), which is clearly better.

As with all things financial, you want to know how the net income is being calculated. Is this an accurate number and is it being calculated on a consistent basis between the two choices? The ROI is a better method of calculation because it includes more information in the decision. The calculation includes the average annual income over the time period that the asset lasts, so we are able to consider the time period beyond when it breaks even. However, keep in mind that you are still making up the numbers for the net income.

Net Present Value (NPV)

NPV techniques involve the time value of money. What this means is that we all more or less agree that a dollar you are going to get in a year is not as valuable to you as a dollar that you have in your wallet right now. The big question is how much less is the dollar in a year worth? The decision comes down to things like inflation and interest rates.

If you could invest a dollar for a year at 20 percent, then the dollar you are waiting for is costing you 20 percent a year. If there is significant inflation, then waiting for a dollar costs you more than if there is no inflation. To use the NPV technique, you need to figure out a discount rate. This is the term for the value you put on having a dollar now rather than later. If inflation is low and your borrowing cost is low, then you will pick a low discount rate. There are tables called present value tables, for obvious reasons, that are used to do this type of calculation.

The NPV technique involves figuring out all of the cash that will come into the organization because of the decision being made and all of the cash that will go out of the business and adjusting all of these cash flows to their present values. For example, take a cash flow that is three years out (say $1000) and multiply that dollar amount by the factor that is found on the present value (PV) table on the row for three years under the column for the discount rate that you want to use. If you use 5 percent for 3 years you will see the factor is .864. This means that $1000 you are going to receive in 3 years has a present value of $864 if 5 percent is the correct rate.

able 33. Example of a table used to calculate present values

7 i	4%	5%	6%	7%	8%	9%	10%	11%	12%	13%
	0.962	0.952	0.943	0.935	0.926	0.917	0.909	0.901	0.893	0.885
	0.925	0.907	0.89	0.873	0.857	0.842	0.826	0.812	0.797	0.783
	0.889	**0.864**	0.840	0.816	0.794	0.772	0.751	0.731	0.712	0.693
	0.855	0.823	0.792	0.763	0.735	0.708	0.683	0.659	0.636	0.613
	0.822	0.784	0.747	0.713	0.681	0.650	0.621	0.593	0.567	0.543
	0.790	0.746	0.705	0.666	0.630	0.596	0.564	0.535	0.507	0.480
	0.760	0.711	0.665	0.623	0.583	0.547	0.513	0.482	0.452	0.425
	0.731	0.677	0.627	0.582	0.540	0.502	0.467	0.434	0.404	0.376
	0.703	0.645	0.592	0.544	0.500	0.460	0.424	0.391	0.361	0.333
	0.676	0.614	0.558	0.508	0.463	0.422	0.386	0.352	0.322	0.295
	0.650	0.585	0.527	0.475	0.429	0.388	0.350	0.317	0.287	0.261
	0.625	0.557	0.497	0.444	0.397	0.356	0.319	0.286	0.257	0.231
	0.601	0.530	0.469	0.415	0.368	0.326	0.290	0.258	0.229	0.204
	0.577	0.505	0.442	0.388	0.340	0.299	0.263	0.232	0.205	0.181
	0.555	0.481	0.417	0.362	0.315	0.275	0.239	0.209	0.183	0.160
	0.534	0.458	0.394	0.339	0.292	0.252	0.218	0.188	0.163	0.142
	0.513	0.436	0.371	0.317	0.270	0.231	0.198	0.170	0.146	0.125
	0.494	0.416	0.350	0.296	0.250	0.212	0.180	0.153	0.130	0.111
	0.475	0.396	0.331	0.277	0.232	0.194	0.164	0.138	0.116	0.098
	0.456	0.377	0.312	0.258	0.215	0.178	0.149	0.124	0.104	0.087

Step one—take all of the cash flow over the lifetime of the capital item and adjust it to the actual present value by multiplying by the correct factor in the table.

Step two—add up the cash inflow.

Step three—subtract the cash outflow from the adjusted cash inflow. If you end up with a positive number, you decide to do the project.

Now you see why payback is the most popular calculation! This NPV stuff is complicated.

Conclusion

When your organization is faced with the decision about which capital item should be purchased, these are the techniques that are used. Each organization sets a policy about which technique is most appropriate and hopefully keeps in mind that the assumptions being made are merely predictions.

Notes and Doodles

Appendix A—Ten Steps to Reviewing Financial Statements

Does the balance sheet balance? Are there two double underlined numbers that are exactly the same? If you are presented with financial statements and the balance sheet does not balance then you should return these financial statements to the person who handed them to you. There is no chance that a balance sheet that does not balance is correct.

Is the retained earnings number on the bottom of the income statement the same as the number on the balance sheet? If not, look no further. The income statement and the balance sheet contain all of the results of the businesses operations. As such, these statements must balance.

Does the business have any cash? Owners care whether or not their business has cash because without cash, payments cannot be made to the employees and the suppliers of the business. It is possible that the business has available credit such as a line of credit that will allow payments to be made. The more cash an organization has, the more comfortable a reader will feel about its ability to pay their bills.

Does the business have equity—that is, are liabilities less than assets? It is important that an organization have equity. If the organization has net liabilities it means the organization owes more than it has. In this situation, who is responsible for paying any liabilities that the business cannot pay? It is possible these creditors will look to the directors to answer this question.

Does the organization have more current assets than current liabilities? This is a test of solvency and can be a requirement of any lenders the business may be dealing with. The comparison of current assets with current liabilities is called the current ratio and is the world's most popular ratio. You want this ratio to be one or more, which means the business has at least as many current assets as current liabilities. The current assets are those assets that will turn into cash within a year, and the current liabilities are those liabilities that must be paid within the year.

How is the business financed? Debt, equity, or a combination? A new business is probably financed entirely with debt. It takes time to build up some equity, which is typically done by making more money that you remove from a business for a number of years.

Has the business made money—that is, is there an excess of revenues over expenses? This information is found on the income statement. You are looking for the revenues to be a larger number than the expenses. It is important that a business make money—that there are more revenues than expenses.

A business is quite interested in making money and the income statement should show that a profit is being made. However, a business is able to run a deficit for a period of time, as the business will have assets that can be pledged to allow borrowing to take place to fund a deficit. A business can take a longer-term view than an NPO. There may also be a comparison to budget on the income statement and if so, you will be able to see if the business achieved its profitability goals as budgeted.

Do any of the expense numbers appear unusually large or small? You have an idea of how much the organization is spending in most areas of the operation. Do you see any expense numbers that do not make sense to you, based on this knowledge? If so, you need to speak up and ask the question.

Are there any expenses you would expect to see and you don't? Before you look at the financial statements, take a moment and try to imagine what you expect to see. It is easy to review what is on the statements, but you might do a better review if you first think about what should be on the statements. Then, if there is anything missing, you are more likely to notice it.

If there are comparative figures, look across each line to see if the financial position has improved or deteriorated. The comparative figures are shown so that the users of the financial statements will have additional information. The questions tend to be things like— why did the organization spend more money on office supplies this year than last? Or why has our insurance increased by so much? The answers will give you a better understanding of the operation of the organization.

Appendix B—Financial Instruments

Financial instruments sound like something exotic and some of them are, things like interest rate swaps and hedges, but more financial instruments are simple things like common shares, bonds, accounts receivable, cash, accounts payable, accounts receivable, and bank loans.

Any financial instrument that is publicly traded must always be shown on a balance sheet at its fair value. Since the fair value is readily obtainable, then that value is relevant to the financial statement readers. As discussed in chapter 7, when we change a number on the balance sheet to reflect its fair value, we have to change another number on the financial statements in order for them to remain in balance. The category on the balance sheet that we use to reflect the changes in value is called accumulated other comprehensive income.

These tables show the balance sheet with an investment shown at cost of $200,000 and the equity section shows the accumulated other comprehensive income at zero. The second table shows the balance sheet with the investments restated at $250,000 and the balancing figure in accumulated other comprehensive income.

Example of a balance sheet before AOCI

Bob's Big Business
BALANCE SHEET

ASSETS

CURRENT

Cash	$57,000
Investments	200,000
Inventory	47,000
	304,000
Fixed assets (Note 1)	158,000
Intangible assets	12,000
	$474,000

LIABILITIES

CURRENT

Accounts payable	$89,103
Demand loan	42,897
HST payable	6,000
Current portion of long-term debt	25,000
	163,000

LONG-TERM

Mortgage	300,000
	463,000

EQUITY

Capital stock	1,000
Accumulated other comprehensive income	0
Retained earnings	10,000
	11,000
	$474,000

Example of a balance sheet with AOCI

Bob's Big Business
BALANCE SHEET

ASSETS

CURRENT

Cash	$57,000
Investments	250,000
Inventory	47,000
	354,000
Fixed assets (Note 1)	158,000
Intangible assets	12,000
	$524,000

LIABILITIES

CURRENT

Accounts payable	$89,103
Demand loan	42,897
HST payable	6,000
Current portion of long-term debt	25,000
	163,000

LONG-TERM

Mortgage	300,000
	463,000

EQUITY

Capital stock	1,000
Accumulated other comprehensive income	50,000
Retained earnings	10,000
	61,000
	$524,000

The term financial instrument has come to mean complicated financial transactions because of the new accounting principles that require that all financial instruments be initially recorded at fair value. This seems like a good idea and why would we want to do anything differently than fair?

The difficulty comes with the definition of fair value. We often define fair value to mean the amount that one person would pay to another for a product or service assuming they are acting at arms-length with no compulsion to act. This is the standard definition of fair market value. For many financial instruments, it is possible to determine fair market value simply by looking in a newspaper or an online reference. Many financial instruments such as publicly traded shares are fairly easy to value because there is an established market for these products. You can sell many shares for their trading value on an exchange.

There are some financial instruments where the fair value may be more difficult to determine. A common example is the interest-free loan. Some car dealers have promotions where they sell a car for the sticker price and do not charge interest on the payments made over the next three or four years.

The accounting standards people cleverly deduce that if you were to offer these car dealers a cash payment instead of taking the interest-free loan, they would reduce the sticker price for the car. So for example a $20,000 car for sale with an interest-free loan over four years might be sold for $16,000 if the buyer offered all of the cash at once. This means that the car is really worth only $16,000 and when the buyer pays back $20,000, the $4000 would be recorded as interest. So if this is really the case, then the fair value of the car loan is only $16,000. You can see how this causes trouble because this would result in a $16,000 car and a $16,000 loan being recorded. Most people would be confused because all of the paper work says that the car cost $20,000.

The fair value rule that requires us to record all assets at fair value also requires us to record that car and the loan at $16,000 on the official books. We would also be required to create an amortization schedule, which would determine the amount of each payment that is interest and which part is principal. You can probably see that there is going to be a conceptual problem with the interest expense as the dealer has stated that it is an interest-free loan. For a taxable organization, this deemed interest expense is not going to be a deduction for tax purposes, the tax return is going to show an asset purchased for $20,000 and amortized that way. The financial statements are going to show a $16,000 asset and interest expense.

When the financial instruments accounting pronouncements came out many accountants rebelled and said that this type of accounting standard does more to confuse the users of financial statements than it does to help them.

Government Loans to Non-Profit Organizations (NPOs)

There is a similar problem with interest-free or low-interest loans being offered to NPOs by funders. In this case the deemed "interest" is treated as government assistance. The theory here is that if an organization is offered a no-interest loan it is a form of government assistance. My thoughts are that we can agree that this is government assistance, but could we not just make a note to the financials? Why do we have to try and quantify the value of a low interest loan?

It can be very challenging to figure out how much an NPO would have been charged for a loan if you consider that it is possible that no loan giving institution would have given this loan. Many NPOs do not meet any credit criteria for getting loans, so the interest rate that would be charged would be very high, say 15 percent to 20 percent. This means that the "deemed interest" is also very high so the effect of this policy is to distort what many people would see as actual results.

Conclusion

The accounting rules around financial instruments are new and complicated.

If your organization is following any generally accepted accounting principles, ASPE, IFRS or ASNPO, then any investments you have that are publicly traded or any low-interest loans will have to be accounted for in accordance with these rules for financial instruments. You will want to have clearly worded policies so that the financial statement readers are able to understand the assumptions used to prepare the financial statements.

Notes and Doodles

Appendix C—Profitability Checklists

Checklist of Strategies for Increasing the Revenue of Your Business

THE STRATEGY	DETAILS	APPLY THE STRATEGY TO YOUR BUSINESS
Increase the price for existing services or products.	Check out your competition. Could your prices be higher? Would higher prices make your market think you have a better product? Do you have better product? If so higher prices are in order!	
Sell more products or services to each existing customer.	What else could your existing customers buy from you? Brainstorm here. Keep your eyes open for opportunities.	
Find more customers.	Never stop marketing. Consider social media and traditional advertising. Where does your target market hangout? Go there!	
Find other products or services that can be sold for higher profits.	Are there complementary products or additional product lines you could add? This strategy can help you find different customers.	
Find other ways to position your services or products to appeal to other target markets.	Could you expand to other geographical areas? Are there other channels you could consider? Wholesalers or other partners? Retailers or direct sales?	
Make full use of the internet. Newsletters, mailing lists, etc.	Are you using your website to the best of its ability? Do you send out your newsletter regularly? Do you blog? Do you tweet? Do you know what I am talking about?	

Checklist of Strategies for Decreasing the Expenses of Your Business

THE STRATEGY	DETAILS	APPLY THE STRATEGY TO YOUR BUSINESS
Buy less expensive products?	Are there products or services that are cheaper but just as good or good enough? Think private label.	
Use less product?	The 'reduce, reuse and recycle' mantra could come in handy here. Look for opportunities to use less of all your materials.	
Do things within the business rather than contracting out?	What is your business particularly good at? Are you taking advantage of these skills? Could you do just as good a job at a cheaper price?	
Subcontract rather than hiring employees?	What is your business not particularly good at? If there are areas where other companies are able to perform some services cheaper and better than you, what are you waiting for? Hire them and spend your time doing stuff you are good at.	
Purchase on consignment?	How much would your suppliers want to change you for products if you bought on consignment? This strategy means that you only pay for products when you sell them. Generally suppliers want more money, but if you are unable to sell the products they cost you nothing. This takes the risk out of purchasing and you can have your store full of products.	
Negotiate better deals with suppliers?	It never hurts to ask. If you do not ask, it is unlikely that anyone is going to volunteer to give you a better deal.	
Review your financial statements more frequently to understand your costs.	Sometimes people are amazed at what they are paying out for expenses. If you do not look, you will never know. Pay attention to your actual numbers and take action when you need to.	
Ask for quotes.	If you ask for a quote, suppliers will know that you are price conscious. If you do not ask for a quote, you may be charged a higher price.	
Set a budget and review it frequently.	Make a plan and stick to it. Don't spend money on impulse in your business or personal life.	

Painless Financial
TRAINING GROUP

Thank you for reading this book. As with most things, there is still much to learn and to remember. Please subscribe to my website (I provide all of the content):

www.PainlessFinancialLearning.ca

Here you will find access to articles, videos, checklists and a weekly tip to inform you on the latest trends, upcoming deadlines and events. This website will help you stay out of trouble and make more money!